BRITISH MILITARY MEDALS

A GUIDE FOR THE COLLECTOR AND FAMILY HISTORIAN

Peter Duckers

Pen & Sword
FAMILY HISTORY

First published in Great Britain in 2009 by
PEN & SWORD FAMILY HISTORY
an imprint of
Pen & Sword Books Ltd
47 Church Street
Barnsley
South Yorkshire
S70 2AS

ISBN 978 1 84415 960 4

Printed and bound in Thailand
by Kyodo Nation Printing Service, Thailand

Pen & Sword Books Ltd incorporates the Imprints of Pen & Sword Aviation,
Pen & Sword Maritime, Pen & Sword Military, Wharncliffe Local History, Pen
and Sword Select, Pen and Sword Military Classics, Leo Cooper, Remember
When, Seaforth Publishing and Frontline Publishing.

For a complete list of Pen & Sword titles please contact

47 Chur   England

CONTENTS

ACKNOWLEDGEMENTS

Some of the photographs used in the text are taken from the author's collection or from that in the Shropshire Regimental Museum in Shrewsbury Castle, used by kind permission of the Trustees. Images of National Archives documents from WO.97, WO.100, ADM.188 and the Medal Index Card are copyright of The National Archives and used with permission. However, many of the photos have been provided by the auction house Messrs Morton and Eden, 45, Maddox Street, London, to whom the author extends his sincere thanks.

INTRODUCTION

Official campaign medals (i.e. those granted simply for service in active operations) and decorations for gallantry have been awarded for well over 150 years. They have been collected for just about as long – at least from the late 1850s when sufficient numbers had been issued to make collecting them a practical possibility. In the earliest days of the hobby, and well into the twentieth century, collectors tended to concentrate on 'types' – trying to obtain one of each type of medal or clasp to form a representative collection of the medals that had been issued. Collections of course varied. Some concentrated on particular campaigns (e.g. the Zulu War), while others were more specific, covering the military history of one regiment, ship or unit; some were regional, covering campaigns or actions in one area (like China or India). More recently, however, the hobby has concentrated on researching the recipient of the award and now constitutes almost a branch of genealogy, where the medal is often simply the starting point for a research project that seeks to outline and commemorate the entire career of the recipient rather than just participation in one campaign or battle.

Similarly, many families find that they have gallantry awards, medals and medal groups relating to members of their own family, sometimes dating back over generations. This is commonly the case with medals for the World Wars of 1914–18 and 1939–45; few families escaped some military involvement in the great conflicts of the twentieth century.

The medallic awards of Britain's military and imperial history provide a tangible and often emotive link with the events of the past – they were issued to and worn by men or women who were actually 'there' and in many cases are the only physical reminder of a person's presence in a particular incident or campaign. Thus we have a real link with an individual who was present at a famous historical event, like the Battle of Waterloo, the Charge of the Light Brigade, the Battle of the Somme or the Battle of Britain, to name only a few. Equally, family medals might relate to campaigns and incidents now long forgotten, like small-scale 'expeditions' in Africa or on the North West Frontier of India.

Whether it is as a hobby or as part of a family history project, researching medals and awards recalls and perpetuates the memory of the men and women, of whatever rank and status, who served their country in their time; they provide both a physical reminder of these people and a memory of their service.

This book examines the origins and development of official campaign, long-service and gallantry awards and offers directions to help in researching them.

Chapter One

CAMPAIGN MEDALS: EARLY HISTORY

Nowadays, we take it for granted that forces' personnel serving on active military operations will receive a campaign medal – if the operations are deemed to be of significance or of some duration. A campaign medal is an award conferred by the government simply for 'being there' – given to all those present in a specific area for a designated length of time and awarded regardless of rank, status or distinction. They are in their simplest form a token of appreciation for services rendered and an official commemoration of one's presence in military operations. British forces may also receive and wear medals awarded by the United Nations or NATO for service under the command of these organisations all over the world.

Today, the process of creating and distributing campaign medals is well established and the awards themselves are standardised in shape, size and look. But this formalised procedure has not always existed and for generations British forces participating in campaigns, large or small, received no general award for their services.

It is usual to identify the awards associated with the Armada campaign of 1588 as the earliest form of campaign medal. Several different types are known, some bearing the effigy of Elizabeth I created by the renowned miniaturist Nicholas Hilliard, who was responsible for much of the official iconography, or 'public face' of the Queen. These beautiful medals are, not surprisingly, excessively rare but there is some doubt as to what they were actually for. They are commonly regarded as rewards given to senior naval commanders in the fleet that fought the Armada in the summer of 1588 (men like Lord Howard, Drake or Raleigh), but the simple fact is that we do not know who actually got them, how many were awarded or what exactly they were awarded for. Some scholars regard the medals as simple commemoratives – celebrating the survival of the Elizabethan Protestant state at a time of religious turmoil and foreign threat. Similarly, medals once regarded as 'naval rewards' that exist from the reign of James I may simply be royal tokens of regard and not specifically campaign awards as we would understand them.

The Civil Wars of 1642–51 gave plenty of scope for a system of campaign medals to develop and there was indeed a range of medals produced during those years. The majority were commissioned and awarded by individual commanders, Parliamentary and Royalist – like the Earl of Essex, Sir Thomas Fairfax or Prince Rupert – or in the name of the King. They were presumably given as rewards to loyal subjects or perhaps for meritorious or gallant service but all are now rare and none conforms to the modern idea of an award issued 'to all those present' at an action or military operation. During the era of the Republic and Commonwealth (1649–58) a variety of naval awards was produced, but again granted sparingly to selected recipients for distinguished service (e.g. against the Dutch) rather than as general rewards.

One of the early awards that perhaps comes closest to the modern concept of general issue was that for the battle of Dunbar in September 1650. Some documentary evidence survives for this medal, which was apparently to be granted to all those serving in Parliament's army under its new Lord General, Oliver Cromwell, which decisively defeated the Scottish Royalist army near Dunbar. Parliament ordered gold and silver medals to be awarded to those present, with designs specially commissioned from the engraver Thomas Simon and featuring a profile of Cromwell. But again, it is not clear exactly how many were issued or to whom. Certainly the originals are now so rare that the possibility of a general award to all the Parliamentary soldiers present (about 13,000) seems unlikely, whatever the original intention of the Commons might have been.

Parliamentary medal for the battle of Dunbar, 1650. Cromwell asked that only Parliament – as the overall source of authority – be shown on the medal, but in the end the Commons decided to add his effigy as Lord General of the forces that decisively defeated the Scots. The medal has some claim to be the first intended general issue.

It remains true that for the rest of the seventeenth century and throughout the eighteenth century there was no national, standardised system of conferring simple campaign medals for war service. Medals were indeed awarded, but they tended to be ad hoc productions, voted to individuals by Parliament, conferred by the King, by local commanders to reward their own men or even produced by associations and societies (such as the Cumberland Society's medal for *Culloden, 1746*). They typically rewarded individual commanders for distinguished leadership or naval officers for gallantry at sea. Many different types were produced over a long period of time, examples being *Admiral Dilkes' Medal* (awarded in gold by Queen Anne to the Admiral and some of his officers for service against the French in July 1703) or the *Louisbourg Medal*, a few of which were awarded in gold, silver or copper (according to rank) for the capture of Louisbourg in Canada in 1756. Many more types were produced as 'medallions', simple commemoratives of victories that could be freely purchased, as souvenir or commemorative tokens rather than official awards for participation in a campaign. The actual concept of giving a medal to every man present on campaign simply did not exist, and this was to remain true well into the nineteenth century.

Examples of Early or Unofficial Awards, 1650–1800

The Commonwealth Naval Medal, 1649–50

This medal may possibly be regarded as the first attempt at a standardised system of awards for distinguished service. In 1649, Parliament decreed that an amount of prize money (from the capture and sale of enemy ships) be set

Above: An example of an unofficial award of the early nineteenth century: Alexander Davison's medal for the battle of Trafalgar, awarded only to the crew of HMS *Victory*. It is one of a number of awards for the battles of the Nile (1798) and Trafalgar (1805) that were financed by private individuals. Medals for Trafalgar were also awarded by the iron-master Matthew Boulton.

aside for the production of medals to reward 'extraordinary service' at sea, initially for actions off Holland. The small, oval medals, designed by Thomas Simon, were struck in gold and silver. They depicted on the obverse shields bearing the Cross of St George (for England) and the Harp of Erin (for Ireland) on either side of an anchor, the whole surrounded by a rope border, below the word *Meruisti* ('You have merited'). The reverse showed Parliament in session in the House of Commons. Original examples are very rare, but later restrikes are known.

The Dunbar Medal, 1651

This oval medal in gold or silver, authorised by Parliament on 7 September 1651, has some claim to being the first 'general issue' of a campaign medal, though it is not clear how many were granted in total or who actually received them. The obverse has the bust of Oliver Cromwell (Parliamentary commander at Dunbar) in armour, with the legend 'The Lord of Hosts' above and 'Word (i.e. password or battle-cry) at Dunbar' to the left and 'Septem: Y 3 1650' to the right. The reverse design, showing Parliament in session, is said to have been suggested by Cromwell himself. This medal was restruck from the original dies in the late eighteenth century, these often showing a clear die flaw. Copies were again produced, from newly cut dies, a hundred years later. Bronze examples are later copies.

The Commonwealth Naval Rewards, 1658

Naval medals were authorised by Parliament in 1658 and issued retrospectively to officers who had rendered distinguished service in campaigns against the Dutch between 1652–54. Three different types are known.

The Toubocanti Medal, 1700

A circular medal in gold or silver was awarded to officers under Captain Campbell who fought the Spanish around the unsuccessful Scottish settlements on the Isthmus of Darien in February 1700. Campbell received a medal in gold; his officers received theirs in silver. They are very rare.

Admiral Dilkes' Gold Medal for Service, 1703

Large gold medals were awarded to Admiral Dilkes and some of his officers for service during the War of the Austrian Succession (1701–14). In July 1703, Dilkes destroyed a French convoy and escorting warships off Cancale Bay. Very few medals were awarded and examples are exceptionally rare.

Medal for the Capture of Louisburg, 1758

Recipients of this medal had taken part in the capture of the French town of Louisbourg in Canada on 27 July 1758 during the Seven Years War. It seems to have been sparingly awarded for gallantry or distinguished services only, rather than as a general 'campaign' award. The medals are sometimes found suspended from a ribbon half yellow and half blue, though originally not intended for wear and issued without suspension.

Medal for the Carib War, 1773

The Legislative Assembly of the Caribbean Island of St Vincent awarded silver medals to local militia and volunteers who suppressed a rebellion by the native Carib inhabitants of the island in 1772–73. The rebellion ended on 20th September 1773 'after a most fatiguing and arduous campaign'. Examples are known in silver, bronze, copper and iron, but it is believed that only silver examples were actually awarded, the others being proofs or presentation pieces. The medal was awarded without ribbon or suspension, but like many early awards, some are seen adapted for wear.

Medals for the Defence of Gibraltar, 1779–93

As a result of the Franco-Spanish siege of Gibraltar between June 1779 and February 1783, a number of unofficial medals were struck to reward those involved in its defence. Some 7,000 British and German forces withstood a 4-year siege, which involved on occasion some serious fighting, and at times held at bay an enemy force of over 60,000 men. The two most frequently seen medals were those presented – and paid for – by the Governor of Gibraltar, General George Eliott (given to his Hanoverian forces) and by General Thomas Picton.

An example of an eighteenth-century 'unofficial' medal: for the Carib War of 1773.

Chapter Two

THE EAST INDIA COMPANY AWARDS AFTER 1784

It was effectively the East India Company (EIC) that began the practice of issuing standardised campaign medals on a large scale. This powerful mercantile company, the instrument of British expansion in India in the late eighteenth century, was anxious to secure the loyalty of its Indian soldiers and had in the past awarded not only medals (in small numbers) but presentation weapons, jewels, money, land or cloth to distinguished soldiers or as rewards for gallantry. By the 1780s the Company was concerned to strengthen the 'ties of loyalty and affection' of its growing Indian forces, who after all were effectively mercenaries fighting for a foreign commercial concern. The EIC originated the idea of awarding each soldier who participated in a campaign a distinctive medal as a token of appreciation 'for services rendered'. The first such award was the *Deccan Medal* of 1784. This was conferred on all the Company's Indian soldiers (but not their British officers and certainly not on British regiments fighting alongside EIC forces) for either or both of two campaigns in India – the First Mahratta War (1780–82) and the Second Mysore campaign (1780–84). The medals established the precedent of conferring awards in different metals (usually gold and silver) and in different sizes according to the rank of the recipient; Indian officers wore theirs around the neck and lower ranks wore them from a cord (later ribbon) on the left breast. The medals were

An early EIC award: the small silver medal for the Mysore campaign of 1790–92. Obverse and reverse shown.

designed by Calcutta silversmiths and produced by the Company's mint in Calcutta. The process of rewarding with a medal every Indian soldier who took part in a significant campaign was maintained by the Company, at considerable expense, through to the end of its existence in 1858, following the 'Indian Mutiny' of 1857–59. There are, therefore, many types of East India Company award that chart the expansion of the Company's (and British) power in India prior to 1857.

Most of these medals are rare and were issued un-named; some were also re-struck in later years, so that they have less of a following among collectors who want original issues or might like to research the career of a particular recipient.

Principal EIC Medals, 1778–1839

It should be noted that with few exceptions (one being the award for Seringapatam in 1799) these medals were only awarded to Indians – not to EIC British officers or to British soldiers.

Medal for the Deccan, 1778–84

Awarded by the EIC for service in operations under Warren Hastings in the Deccan in Western India and Gujerat between 1778–84. Minted in Calcutta, they were awarded in two sizes – 40.5mm in gold and silver and 32mm in silver. The larger medals were given to Indian officers only. They may be regarded as the first 'general issue' war medals.

Medal for the Mysore Campaign, 1790–92

Awarded by the EIC for the campaign of 1790–92 in Mysore against the powerful Tipu Sultan (see also the Seringapatam medal). They were produced in two sizes, 43mm and 38mm, the larger one in gold and silver conferred upon Indian officers and the smaller silver version on the Other Ranks of the Company's Indian forces. (See photograph on p. 16.)

Medal for the Capture of Ceylon, 1795–96

Ceylon was taken from the Dutch at the outset of the French Wars and confirmed as a British possession in 1814. In 1807 the EIC awarded approximately 123 medals to men of the Bengal Artillery who were present at the capture of the island in 1795. Why other units involved were not awarded the medal is unknown.

Medal for the Capture of Seringapatam, 1799

This was authorised in July 1808 for award to EIC forces that took part in the renewed campaign against Tipu Sultan of Mysore. This culminated in the storming of the fortress-city of Seringapatam on 4 May 1799. Medals were awarded in gold, silver-gilt, silver, bronze or pewter according to rank. Much later they were allowed to be worn by EIC and British officers, in 1814 and 1851 respectively.

The Honourable East India Company's Medal for Egypt, 1801

In July 1802 the EIC authorised a medal for service in the Egypt campaign of 1801, though it was not actually issued until 1811. Produced by the Calcutta Mint, it was awarded in gold (16 awarded) and silver (approximately 2,200) and is rare. The medal was not given to British troops, who had to wait until the issue of the *Military General Service Medal* and *Naval General Service Medal* (q.v.) with clasp *Egypt* and then not until 1850, as something of an afterthought.

Medal for the Capture of Rodrigues, the Isle of Bourbon and the Île de France, 1809–10

Awarded by the EIC in 1812 for the capture of the French islands of Rodrigues, Bourbon (now Réunion) and Île de France (now Mauritius) between July 1809 and December 1810. Only 45 were awarded in gold and approximately 2,000 in silver.

Medal for the Capture of Java, 1811

Awarded to EIC forces who took part in the capture of Java in 1811, part of a policy of striking against the Dutch Empire in the Far East. As usual with EIC awards, medals were issued in gold to senior officers and in silver to others. Survivors of the British forces engaged had to wait until 1847 for the award of the *Military General Service Medal* and *Naval General Service Medal* (q.v.) with clasp *Java*.

Above: The EIC medal for Egypt, 1801. The obverse (Shown) depicts a *sepoy* (Indian soldier) holding the Union flag. The inscription in Persian records: 'the great bravery of the victorious army of England', but British soldiers had to wait until 1830 to get a medal..

Medal for the Nepal War, 1814–16

The conquest of the Gurkha kingdom of Nepal necessitated one of hardest campaigns that the EIC and associated British forces had yet experienced. The silver medal, awarded in 1816, was given only to the forces of the EIC and since only about 300 are thought to have been issued, they clearly were not made generally available. British units had to wait until 1851 when survivors were rewarded with the *Army of India Medal* with clasp *Nepaul*.

The Honourable East India Company's Medal for the Ava Campaign, Burma, 1824–26

Awarded in gold, silver-gilt and silver in 1826 to the forces of the EIC for the campaign of 1824–26 in the Kingdom of Ava in lower Burma. It was the first EIC medal to be of the standardised shape and dimensions that became the norm in later medals and copied the clip-and-ring suspension of the *Waterloo Medal (q.v.)*. The ribbon, once called 'the military ribbon of Great Britain' (dark red with blue edges) equally imitated that of the *Waterloo Medal*. Survivors of the British forces engaged had to wait until 1851 and the issue of the *Army of India Medal* with clasp *Ava*.

The Honourable East India Company's Medal for the Coorg Rebellion, 1837

Approved in August 1837, this medal was awarded by the EIC to chiefs and men of the loyal Coorgs who suppressed a rebellion in the Canara district. It is believed that only approximately 345 medals were awarded and these mostly to loyal chiefs and high-ranking officers rather than to lower ranks.

Above: EIC silver medal for the capture of Java, 1811. The obverse, showing the attack on Fort--Cornelis.

Chapter Three

THE EARLIEST BRITISH CAMPAIGN MEDALS, 1815–42

Most books on the subject of British medals accept that the first 'real' campaign medal in the modern sense of an award to all ranks present in a particular action or campaign was that produced for the Waterloo campaign of June 1815. This was indeed the first medal to be issued to all British soldiers, officers and men alike, in a standardised form for all recipients. It was the first British medal to bear the recipient's name and other details (impressed around the rim by a machine designed for this purpose at Matthew Boulton's Soho mint in Birmingham) and was the first medal to be granted to the next of kin of those killed during the campaign, though a special application had to be made in those cases. There is no doubting the *Waterloo Medal*'s status as 'the first British campaign medal' but its award actually reflects the significance attached to the victory itself rather than a general desire on the part of the British government to award medals to soldiers. In fact, for over twenty years after Waterloo, no official British war medals were issued – only the East India Company continued the process of general awards, almost exclusively to its Indian forces, and it was really out of these issues that the modern system evolved.

In 1839, a combined British and EIC army invaded Afghanistan, intending to place on the throne a pro-British ruler, Shah Shujah-ul-Mulk, who would counter the perceived involvement of Russia in Afghan affairs. This army stormed the fortress-city of Ghuznee in July 1839 before going on to occupy Kabul and place Shah Shujah on the throne. In gratitude for this support, the new Emir announced that he would confer a medal on all those troops, British and Indian, who had been present at the taking of Ghuznee. An order for approximately 8,000 medals was accordingly placed with the Calcutta mint.

However, things quickly fell apart. Afghanistan rose up in revolt against foreign occupation, Shah Shujah was killed and the British occupation force in the capital was forced into the disastrous 'retreat from Kabul' in which thousands of British and Indian soldiers and 'followers' were killed or died. The towns of Jellalabad and Khelat-i-Ghilzie were besieged. A major campaign of retribution followed in 1842, with augmented British and Indian forces re-occupying strategic positions in Afghanistan (like Jellalabad, Ghuznee, Kandahar and Kabul) before imposing a peace treaty and then withdrawing from the country.

However, the EIC announced that the original intention of Shah Shujah to reward the forces that had taken Ghuznee in 1839 would be honoured, with the Company taking over the production and distribution of the medal.

And since British troops were included in the original proposal, permission was sought from the home government to grant the *Ghuznee Medal* to the British forces that had been engaged. This permission was granted, since it had been made as a matter of honour by a foreign leader, and British forces duly received the silver medal. This was really the first medal issued to British (as opposed solely to Indian) soldiers since Waterloo. When it then came to issuing a range of medals for service in Afghanistan for the campaigns of 1842, as per usual instituted by the EIC for its Indian forces, there seemed no reason why British forces should not receive these awards and permission to confer the medals on British troops was again sought and again granted.

At the same time that British and Indian forces were engaged in Afghanistan, they were also being deployed in China during the 'Opium War' of 1840–42. The East India Company again

Top right: The obverse (left) and reverse (right) of the *Waterloo Medal*, 1815. The obverse carries the effigy of the Prince Regent, ruling in place of the incapacitated George III since 1812. The reverse design is apparently derived from an ancient Greek coin.

Left: The obverse of the medal for Ghuznee, 1839. A fine depiction of the impressive citadel and its defended gates, stormed by a British-Indian force on 23 July 1839. It was the first EIC medal to be given in quantity to British forces.

proposed a medal for award to its
Indian forces, but simultaneously
the Queen announced that British
naval and land forces would also
receive a medal, initially for
some of the larger actions of the
campaign (e.g. the seizure of
Canton). It was ultimately agreed
that all the forces engaged should get
the same medal, which was duly
awarded as the first *China War
Medal* in 1843. (See photograph on
p. 24)

From this point on, all the
medals instituted by the East India
Company for subsequent campaigns
in India were also awarded to associated
British troops – for the Gwalior and Scinde campaigns of 1843 and for the
two Sikh Wars of 1845–46 and 1848–49. By this time some standardisation
becomes noticeable – medals were (generally) circular, of standardised
dimensions, made of silver and suspended from a coloured ribbon specific
to that award, with the recipient's details (e.g. name, rank and unit)
engraved or impressed around the rim. Since they were now authorised by
the monarch, they bore the sovereign's effigy and titles (typically just
'Victoria Regina' on the early awards) and some symbolic design or simple
wording on the reverse. With the medal for the *1st Sikh War* (the Sutlej

Top right: Medals for the *1st Afghan War*
(reverse, left) and for the *Scinde Campaign* of 1843
(reverse, right). Both bear simple wording record-
ing the areas or battles in which the recipient
served. The ribbon, once known as the 'India
Ribbon' or 'sunrise in the east', was used on many
early Indian medals and was re-used with the
Kabul to Kandahar Star in 1880.

Left: Reverses of the *Sutlej Medal* for the 1st
Sikh War, 1845–46 (left) and for the *Punjab Medal*
for the 2nd Sikh War, 1848–49 (right). The allegorical design on the left is highly regarded for its
artistic merits; that on the right shows Sir Walter
Gilbert receiving the surrender of the Sikh army.

campaign of 1845–46) was born the idea of battle clasps – silver bars added to the medal which carried the name of a particular action singled out for special record. This policy was continued with the subsequent *Punjab Medal* (for the 2nd Sikh War of 1848–49) and thereafter became a standard way of commemorating the recipient's presence in a particularly important victory or campaign down to the present day.

We can therefore date the institution of a standardised system of British campaign medals and clasps to the Afghan, Indian and China Wars of the period 1839–49.

Early Awards and Related Medal Rolls

The Waterloo Medal, 1815

The silver medal awarded for the campaign in the Low Countries in June 1815. Awarded to British and King's German Legion forces present at the battles of Quatre Bras, and/or Waterloo and to reserve forces not actually present at Waterloo (e.g. those based at Hal and Tubize). Regarded as 'the first British war medal'. The original medal rolls for the *Waterloo Medal* are held in The National Archives (TNA) under series WO.100-14 (cavalry, artillery, wagon train and Guards), WO.100-15.1 (British regiments of foot) and WO.100-15.2 (Rifle Brigade, King's German Legion). File MINT.16/112 also has an original *Waterloo Medal* roll.

There are published rolls for this medal:

- *The Waterloo Medal Roll* (Uckfield, Naval and Military Press, 1992)
- *The Waterloo Roll Call*, C Dalton (n.p., 1904; reprinted Uckfield, Arms & Armour Press, 1978): officers and officer casualties.

1st Afghan War: the Ghuznee Medal, 1839

A silver medal awarded to British and EIC forces for the capture of the major fortress-city of Ghuznee (Ghazni) between 21–23 July 1839. No medal roll survives for this award, but a prize roll lists those who received a financial reward for their share in the capture; this effectively identifies those who would have received the medal.

1st Afghan War: Medal for the Defence of Jellalabad, 1841–42

A silver medal awarded by the EIC to the garrison that defended the fortified town of Jellalabad on the Afghan side of the Khyber Pass, 1841–42. Most awards went to the 13th (Somerset) Light Infantry.

1st Type ('mural crown' reverse)
2nd type ('Flying Victory' reverse)
2nd type with 'Victoria Regina' title instead of usual 'Victoria Vindex'

Medal roll: India Office, L.Mil.5-68.

1st Afghan War: Medal for the Defence of Khelat-i-Ghilzie, 1842

This rare silver medal was granted in October 1842 to the small force of approximately 950 Indian soldiers that defended the fortified town of Khelat-i-Ghilzie between Kandahar and Kabul from February to May 1842.
No medal roll survives for this award.

The 1st Afghan War: Medals for Candahar, Ghuznee and Cabul, 1842

Silver medals awarded to EIC and British forces for the re-invasion of Afghanistan in 1842. With various reverses reflecting areas of service:
Candahar-Ghuznee-Cabul
Ghuznee-Cabul
Cabul
Cabvl (rare variant spelling)

No medal roll survives for these awards, but British regimental muster and pay rolls (in series WO.12 at TNA, Kew) will confirm a soldier's presence on campaign.

- *The First Afghan War 1839–42 and its Medals*, A G Stone (London, Spink, 1967).

The China War Medal, 1840–42

The silver medal granted to EIC and British forces engaged in the 'Opium War' or 1st China War of 1840–42. No clasps – but see *China 1856–60* below.

Only fragmentary rolls survive, with little for British regiments, apart from W.O.55-1240 which is a roll for the Royal Artillery. In the India Office Collections, L.Mil.5-67 lists some recipients, largely of the Madras army and L.Mil.66 has recipients in EIC naval forces. Royal Navy recipients are listed in Admiralty files ADM.171-6, ADM.171-7 and ADM.171-12.

Medal for the 1st China War of 1840–42, often called the 'Opium War'.
Obverse showing the 'young head' of Victoria by the leading Royal Mint designer William Wyon used on many campaign medals up to the 1860s.

Chapter Four

THE RETROSPECTIVE MEDALS OF 1847–51

An indication of how far the acceptability of awarding general campaign medals had advanced can be seen by the introduction of a series of 'retrospective' medals in the period 1847–51. For some time it had been felt that the soldiers and sailors of the French Revolutionary and Napoleonic Wars of 1793–1815 – already receding into the past as historical events – should belatedly receive some kind of reward. As a result, three new medals were introduced.

The *Military General Service Medal* (MGS) was instituted in 1847 and awarded to survivors (only) of the land campaigns of 1793–1814. Despite the dates on the medal, its first clasp was for *Egypt* (1801) and most of the other clasps commemorated the great battles of the Peninsular War – like *Corunna* (1809), *Talavera* (1809), *Salamanca* (1812) and *Vittoria* (1813) – and the battles that took the war across the Pyrenees and into Southern France (like *Nive*, *Nivelle*, *Orthes* and *Toulouse*). A few clasps recorded military expeditions and exploits elsewhere – *Martinique*, *Guadeloupe*, *Java* and *Maida* being examples. Perhaps the most sought-after are those that recall the largely forgotten Anglo-American war of 1812–14, fought on the Canadian Frontier: *Fort Detroit*, *Chateauguay* and *Chrystler's Farm*. Some 26,000 survivors received the medal and some claimed up to 14 clasps – though 1 to 5 is more common.

'To the British Army': the *Military General Service Medal* 1847, showing six clasps for the later stages of the Peninsular War, 1813–14. The reverse shows Queen Victoria crowning the Duke of Wellington – though she had not been born at the time of the campaigns and Wellington was not involved in all of them!

Obverse (left) and reverse (right) of the retrospective *Naval General Service Medal* of 1847. This carries the single clasp *Trafalgar* for Nelson's great victory of 21 October 1805.

Since Britain's war effort in the years 1793–1815 was largely naval, the *Naval General Service Medal* (NGS), issued to survivors only, was a much more complicated affair. There were over 240 possible clasps, reflecting naval warfare right around the world. Some clasps recalled the great naval exploits that have become entrenched in British history – like 'the Glorious First of June' (*1st June 1794*) and Nelson's great victories of the *Nile*, *Copenhagen* or *Trafalgar*; others commemorate naval actions in support of land forces, like *St Sebastian, Java, Martinique, Egypt* etc. and some commemorate smaller fleet and squadron actions, like *17th June 1795* or *Basque Roads 1805*. However, the majority of the clasps to the NGS were awarded for ship-to-ship engagements (like *Shannon with Chesapeake*) or boat actions – where the small boats from warships served in attacking shore positions or 'cutting out' or destroying enemy ships in port. Most of the single-ship and 'boat action' clasps are rare as they were only issued in small numbers, since few men were originally involved and even fewer were alive to claim them in 1847.

Unlike the MGS, the NGS was also awarded for actions after 1815 – it was granted with clasp *Algiers* for the expedition against the Barbary pirates in Algiers in 1816, with *Navarino* for the battle that destroyed the Turkish fleet in 1827 and helped secure Greek independence and finally with clasp *Syria* for the extensive operations against Mehemet Ali in the eastern Mediterranean in 1840. Perhaps as a reflection of just how harsh conditions were at sea in those days, there were fewer claimants for the NGS – only 21,000 – and the majority (approximately 15,600) received single-clasp medals, mostly for the post-1815 actions; unlike the MGS, multiple-clasp awards of the NGS are rare.

Somewhat belatedly, it was decided in 1851 to issue an equivalent medal for those who had served in early campaigns in India. The *Army of India Medal* – effectively the first in a long line of 'India General Service' medals (see below) – carried the dates *1799–1826*, but its first actual clasp was for the battle of *Allighur* in 1803. Perhaps the greatest battle commemorated on its twenty-one clasps was Assaye (or *Assye* on the clasp) in 1803 – the first great victory won against incredible odds by the future Duke of Wellington. As with the NGS, the *Army of India Medal* was also awarded for campaigns after 1815 – with clasp *Bhurtpoor* for the siege of that town in 1824 and *Ava* for the full-scale campaign against the kingdom of Ava in southern Burma, 1824–26. Again reflecting the arduous nature of service in India in those days, only approximately 4,500 medals were awarded, with clasps to mere handfuls of surviving claimants, so that some clasps and multi-clasp medals are very rare.

The reverse of the retrospective *Army of India Medal* with the last of its clasps, *Ava*, for service in lower Burma, 1824–26.

The Retrospective Medals and Clasps and their Medal Rolls

The Military General Service Medal, 1847

A retrospective silver medal awarded to *survivors only* for service in the French Revolutionary and Napoleonic Wars. Not awarded without clasp.

Egypt	*Java*
Maida	*Ciudad Rodrigo*
Roleia	*Badajoz*
Vimiera	*Salamanca*
Sahagun	*Fort Detroit*
Benevente	*Chateauguay*
Sahagun & Benevente	*Chrystler's Farm*
Corunna	*Vittoria*
Martinique	*Pyrenees*
Talavera	*St Sebastian*
Guadaloupe	*Nivelle*
Busaco	*Nive*
Barrosa	*Orthes*
Fuentes d'Onor	*Toulouse*
Albuhera	

The original correspondence surrounding the awards and the actual medal rolls for the *Military General Service Medal* are held at TNA in Kew under the following series:

- WO.100, files 1–9 for British Army units
- WO.100, file 10 for miscellaneous foreign corps like the King's German Legion
- WO.100, file 11 for miscellaneous claims to various corps
- WO.100, file 12 for awards of the clasp *Egypt* (1801) – belatedly awarded.

There are published rolls for this medal:

- *The Military General Service Medal, 1793–1814*, Col. O N Kingsley Foster (Berlin, 1947), now largely superseded by:
- *The Military General Service Medal, 1793–1814*, A L T Mullen (London, London Stamp Exchange, 1990)
- *The Three Great Retrospective Medals, 1793–1840 awarded to the Royal Artillery*, Lt Col. D D Vigors (privately published, 1986).

The Naval General Service Medal, 1793–1840

Instituted in 1847 for issue to *survivors only* of naval campaigns and actions from 1793 and extended to 1840. Never issued without clasp, of which a *selection* is listed below, with numbers awarded:

Fleet Actions

1 June 1794 (540)

14 March 1795 (95)

23 June 1795 (177)

St Vincent (348)

Camperdown (298)

Nile (336)

Egypt (618)

Copenhagen 1801 (555)

Trafalgar (1,710)

4 Novr 1805 (296)

Martinique (486)

Basque Roads (529)

Guadaloupe (483)

Java (665)

St Domingo (396)

St Sebastian (293)

Algiers (1,328)

Navarino (1,142)

Syria (6,978)

Frigate Actions

Mars 21 April 1798 (26)

Lion 15 July 1798 (23)

Acre 30 May 1799 (41)

London 13 March 1806 (27)

Curacao 1 Jany 1807 (65)

Stately 22 March 1808 (31)

Lissa (124)

Gut of Gibraltar (142)

Boat Service

16 July 1805 (51)

1 Novr 1809 (110)

28 June 1810 (25)

29 Sept 1812 (25)

2 May 1813 (48)

8 April 1814 (24)

14 Decr 1814 (205)

The original correspondence surrounding the awards and the actual medal rolls for the *Naval General Service Medal*, are held at TNA in Kew under the following Admiralty series:

- ADM.171-1 for clasps relating to actions up to 1815
- ADM.171-4 for the clasp *Algiers* (1816)
- ADM.171-5 for the clasp *Navarino* (1826)
- ADM.171-6 for the clasp *Syria* (1840)
- also ADM.171-8 and 171–94.

There are published rolls for this medal:

- *Naval General Service Medal Rolls, 1793–1840*, Capt. K Douglas-Morris (privately published, 1982)
- *Alphabetical Naval General Service Medal, 1793–1840*, C S Message (Suffolk, 1996)
- *The Naval Biographical Dictionary*, W O'Byrne (n.p., 1849; reprinted): officers' careers
- *The Trafalgar Roll: Ships and Officers*, Col. R H Mackenzie (n.p., 1989).

The Army of India Medal, 1851: to EIC and British Troops

A silver medal awarded to *survivors only*, British and Indian, for early campaigns in India. Not awarded without clasp:

Allighur	*Kirkee*
Battle of Delhi	*Poona*
Assye	*Kirkee & Poona*
Asserghur	*Seetabuldee*
Laswarree	*Nagpore*
Argaum	*Seetabuldee & Nagpore*
Gawilghur	*Maheidpoor*
Defence of Delhi	*Corygaum*
Battle of Deig	*Ava*
Capture of Deig	*Bhurtpoor*
Nepaul	

Medal rolls:

- WO.100-13: rolls for British regiments claiming awards
- ADM.171-11: roll of naval claimants for the clasp *Ava* (Burma, 1824–26).

Correspondence and rolls (largely for Indian regiments engaged) are also held in the India Office Collection at the British Library in L.Mil.5, files 42, 43, 44. It should be noted that these rolls do not include Indian recipients, for whom lists no longer survive. They only relate to British officers and British soldiers serving in Indian regiments.

There are published rolls for this medal:

- *The Army of India Medal Roll*, R J Gould and Capt. J K Douglas-Morris (London, Hayward, 1974)
- *The Three Great Retrospective Medals, 1793–1840 awarded to the Royal Artillery*, Lt Col. D D Vigors (n.p., 1986).

Chapter Five

MEDALS FOR MAJOR CAMPAIGNS, 1850–1914

Once the idea of standardised awards had become established by 1850, all the major conflicts in which British forces were henceforward employed were commemorated with a distinctive medal.

Britain's first war against a major European power since 1815, the Russian War of 1854–56 (now better known as the Crimean War because of the land campaign waged there) produced two medals. The *Baltic Medal 1854–55* was awarded mainly to Royal Navy and Royal Marine forces engaged in the campaign in the Gulf of Finland and apart from one major incident, the attack on the fortress of Bomarsund on the Aaland Islands, mainly involved the use of small landing parties attacking coastal defences and depots and a blockade of Russian shipping and naval bases, such as Kronstadt. No clasps were issued with this medal, which was awarded un-named, apart from a few to Army sappers and miners serving with the naval force. Un-named medals tend to attract less interest simply because they have no researchable link with an individual, unless they are part of a larger group containing named awards. Many are found privately engraved, but as with all such medals the collector needs to be sure that the naming style is contemporary and not something added later to increase the value of the medal.

The campaign in the Crimea produced a medal that carried distinctive clasps in the shape of oak leaves with acorns. Nowadays regarded as elegant and attractive, they caused some adverse comment at the time, being regarded by some as 'unmilitary', and the design was never re-used. Clasps were issued to commemorate

Medal for the Baltic Campaign, 1854–55 – an extensive naval campaign during the Russian War, now largely forgotten. The reverse shows a seated Britannia, with the fortress of Bomarsund in the left background. Commonly found unnamed or privately engraved, very few were officially named.

the great set battles of the war – *Alma* (20 September 1854), *Balaklava* (25 October 1854) and *Inkermann* (5 November 1854) – and the arduous siege of *Sebastopol* prior to the fall of the port in September 1855. Medals were also awarded to Royal Navy and Royal Marine personnel, without clasps for service offshore or around the Black Sea or with clasps for those who landed as part of naval brigades and served in land operations. Many naval awards were given, for example, to sailors and marines manning siege guns landed from the fleet to serve 'before Sebastopol' or for the naval bombardment of the port. A purely naval clasp, *Azoff*, was granted to naval and marine forces for the successful naval campaign in the Sea of Azoff in 1855. Nowadays, however, the campaign is remembered (if at all) not for successful battles that defeated the Russians in the field or at sea but for its 'glorious failures' like the Charge of the Light Brigade on 25 October 1854 and for the terrible suffering of British soldiers in the Russian winter, the unsatisfactory organisation of food, equipment and supplies and for the poor treatment of the wounded and sick.

Most Crimean War medals were issued un-named, since the authorities were anxious to reward British forces during what had been an unpopular campaign and get the medals out to the troops 'in the field' very quickly; those officially named at the Royal Mint usually went to the next of kin of casualties, to recipients who made a special point of having their medal returned to be officially named or to the crews of four warships that had returned from the Black Sea at the time the medals were being issued (viz. HMS *London*, *Rodney*, *Wasp* and *Niger* – though the ship is not named on the medal). However, many regiments and men personalised the medals by having them regimentally impressed or privately engraved, so that a wide range of naming styles can be found on Crimean and Baltic medals. Since some can be very expensive on the collectors' market – especially those to men who served in the Charge of the Light Brigade at Balaklava or

Above: *Medal for the Crimean Campaign, 1854–56, with three clasps – Alma, Inkermann and Sebastopol. Reverse, showing Victory crowning a Roman soldier. The attractive design of the clasps, decorated with oak leaves and acorns, was never used again.*

in 'the Thin Red Line' in defence of the same port –
it is important for the collector to know which
naming styles are appropriate to the period and not
fraudulently added later to increase the value of an
otherwise un-named medal.

Since Britain was fighting on behalf of the
Ottoman Empire, the Sultan awarded Turkish
medals to all those who were engaged in the
Crimea prior to the fall of Sebastopol, so that
British personnel received two medals for their
war service. The *Turkish Crimean Medals*, awarded in
silver, bore three different reverse inscriptions – in
French, in Italian (for the Sardinian forces engaged)
and in English, but most British recipients received
the Italian version following the loss at sea of a
ship carrying the consignment of the British type.
Originally suspended from small rings via a
narrow half-width ribbon, most are found with
altered suspensions and wider ribbons, to match
the British awards worn with them.

An equally arduous campaign is commemorated
by the *Indian Mutiny Medal* (1857–59), of which nearly
300,000 were issued. This was the last award proposed by
the East India Company, though in the event its manufacture and
issue were taken over by the British government following the demise of the
EIC in 1858. Its clasps commemorate some really hard fighting. *Delhi* was
awarded to the comparatively small force of British and loyal Indian troops
that endured the long siege of Delhi Ridge from June–September and then
stormed the revived Mogul capital in September 1857. The force was almost
overwhelmed during the siege and its military achievement in taking so
great a city against so large an enemy is quite remarkable. The rarest clasp
is *Defence of Lucknow*. These are specially prized to those who took part in
the original defence from June to September 1857, especially the
32nd Regiment, and to the large number of Indians who remained loyal and
served throughout the siege. It was also awarded to the men of the 1st Relief
Force under Sir Henry Havelock which fought its way into the city in
September 1857 but could not then remove the garrison (with its large
complement of civilians, including women, children and wounded) and

Above: The Turkish medal for the Crimea, showing the British reverse. As is common,
this example has had the suspension altered to match other British awards.

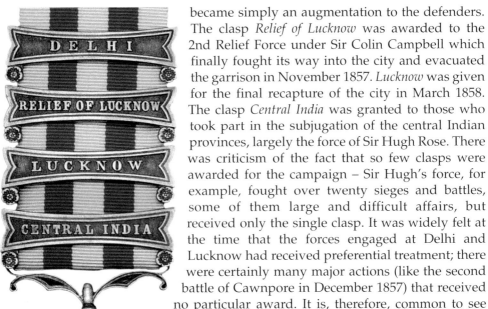

became simply an augmentation to the defenders. The clasp *Relief of Lucknow* was awarded to the 2nd Relief Force under Sir Colin Campbell which finally fought its way into the city and evacuated the garrison in November 1857. *Lucknow* was given for the final recapture of the city in March 1858. The clasp *Central India* was granted to those who took part in the subjugation of the central Indian provinces, largely the force of Sir Hugh Rose. There was criticism of the fact that so few clasps were awarded for the campaign – Sir Hugh's force, for example, fought over twenty sieges and battles, some of them large and difficult affairs, but received only the single clasp. It was widely felt at the time that the forces engaged at Delhi and Lucknow had received preferential treatment; there were certainly many major actions (like the second battle of Cawnpore in December 1857) that received no particular award. It is, therefore, common to see the *Indian Mutiny Medal* with no clasp – the only reward that soldiers received for sometimes arduous and protracted service, but not in the main 'theatres' of Delhi, Lucknow or Central India. Medals awarded to the naval brigades drawn from HMS *Shannon* and *Pearl* – landed in Calcutta at a time when there was a desperate shortage of men and heavy guns and which saw some arduous service – are particularly collected, as are the multi-clasp awards to the 9th Lancers and Bengal Horse Artillery. Some of the latter were the only ones to receive four clasps – *Delhi, Relief of Lucknow, Lucknow, Central India* – the maximum possible for the campaign.

Throughout the nineteenth century, participation in larger wars – those involving significant forces over longer periods of time – continued to be rewarded with their own distinctive campaign medals. Examples of regional awards that might also be considered as 'general service' medals were those issued for the successive China Wars between 1840–1900, which use the same basic reverse design of a 'trophy of arms' and carried the same

Above: The *Indian Mutiny Medal*, reverse, with four of the five clasps awarded for the campaign – the maximum possible for one recipient. It has a 'cusped suspension' and 'fish-tail' clasps, used only on this award and that for the contemporary 2nd China War (see p. 35).

ribbon. The first such medal was awarded for the 1st China War (or 'Opium War') between 1840 and 1842 and carried no clasps. For the Anglo-French campaign generally known as the 2nd China War (actually split into two distinct phases, 1856–58 and 1860) the same basic design was approved. In this case, however, a swivelling 'cusped' suspension and 'fish-tail' clasps (as on the contemporary *Indian Mutiny Medal*) were used. Clasps were issued for the furious naval action at *Fatshan 1857* and for the capture of the major city of Canton (*Canton 1857*). Two clasps were awarded for the successive attacks on the Taku Forts at the mouth of the Peiho River – both strongly contested engagements – with *Taku Forts 1858* and/or *Taku Forts 1860*. The final clasp was *Pekin 1860*, awarded for the military occupation of the capital, an occupation noted for the looting and destruction of the Imperial Summer Palace by British and French troops. The medal was also awarded without clasps to naval forces operating off the Chinese coast and also involved in the extensive Taeping rebellion, which shook imperial China until 1864. The final appearance of the standard China War design came with the 3rd China War or 'Boxer Rebellion' in 1900. This campaign was most unusual in involving a large international force – representing powers with vested interests in Chinese trade and controlling various 'Treaty Ports' along the Chinese coast. These included (apart from Great Britain), France, Italy, Russia, Austria, Japan, Germany and the USA and all issued their own medals for the campaign. The result was complicated operations involving mixed international forces, technically under German overall command. The *1900 China Medal* was issued with only three clasps. By far the rarest – and one of the rarest of all British clasps – was *Defence of Legations*, awarded to embassy staffs, civilian volunteers and embassy guards (mainly Royal Marines in the case of the British embassy) which were besieged in Peking for fifty-five days in 1900. *Taku Forts* was given for the further naval attacks on the forts in Peiho entrance (and only granted to Royal Navy and Royal Marine forces), and

Above: Medal for the 2nd China War (1856–60) with examples of two clasps. The medal bore essentially the same reverse (shown) as that for China, 1840–42 and for China, 1900 – a 'trophy of arms' under the motto '*Armis Exposcere Pacem*' ('to achieve peace by force of arms') – and carried the same ribbon for each campaign.

Relief of Pekin to those naval, marine and military forces (British and Indian) engaged in the march to Peking, the relief of the besieged embassies and the occupation of the capital. The medal is commonly seen with no clasp, to naval personnel based offshore or to the many British and Indian soldiers who served ashore after the relief of Pekin or at other places along the extensive Chinese coast or inland. Active operations did not end until 1901.

One of the more unusual and complicated of nineteenth-century medals was that awarded for the various *Maori Wars* in New Zealand between 1845–46 and 1860–66. Only authorised in 1869, the medal carried no clasps but bore the dates of the recipient's service on the reverse (e.g. '1845–47', '1860–61' etc.). Those awarded to Royal Navy and Royal Marine forces were only given to those who landed and were actually engaged in land operations – they were not granted to those who simply served on warships off the coast, as was the case with some later medals (e.g. for Ashanti 1873–74, South Africa 1877–79 or Egypt 1882–85). This means that naval awards are rather unusual and there are also some combinations of dates that are rare to certain units. This policy of identifying the actual dates served on the reverse of the medal meant that there are no fewer than six different reverses covering the period 1845–47 and twenty-two for the period 1860–66. Some were also awarded with no dates on the reverse. They can be found not only to British military and naval forces but also to a plethora of local volunteers and militias. Many of these forces continued to be 'actively engaged' up to 1880, long after British forces had been permanently withdrawn from New Zealand.

Perhaps the most unusual British campaign medal was that awarded for the Abyssinia campaign of 1868. This was one of the most successful and well organised of Victorian campaigns, which achieved its aim (the release of hostages) with few British casualties. There were no famous disasters or victories – just Lord Napier's well-planned strike against Magdala, the fortress-city of King Theodore. British and Indian land and naval units received the medal, which was highly distinctive. Apart from its strikingly original design, the medal has gone on record as the most expensive ever

Above: The silver medal for the New Zealand or Maori Wars, 1845–66. Issued without clasps, the medal bore a wide range of dates, in this case reflecting service only in 1866. The suspension, unique to this issue, is decorated with the New Zealand fern leaf.

produced since the majority (apart from most of those to Indian troops) were awarded with the recipient's name and details embossed onto a plate on the reverse – which meant that a separate die had to be produced for each of approximately 14,000 medals. This procedure was never repeated!

The difficult campaign of June 1873–February 1874 against the Ashanti Empire in West Africa (or Ashantee, as it was then spelled) produced what is generally regarded as one of the most detailed and attractive of medal reverses. It depicts close fighting in the West African forest and is very finely worked. It serves to remind us that some awards have a real aesthetic aspect which is often neglected these days; other medals with reverse designs that have been particularly praised for their artistic qualities are the *Sutlej Medal* of 1845–46 and the *Sudan Medal* of 1896–98. The *Ashantee War Medal* was awarded to naval forces that bore the brunt of the fighting early in the campaign – defending coastal settlements against Ashanti attacks – and to the military and naval forces later employed under Sir Garnet Wolseley.

These fought their way inland, crossed the Prah and fought the Ashanti before occupying their capital Coomassie (as then spelled) and imposing a treaty on the Ashanti king, Kofi. Apart from a severe engagement at Amoaful, tropical disease and the difficult jungle terrain inflicted most of the casualties. The clasp *Coomassie* was granted to those who were present at Amoaful on 31 January 1874 and in the occupation of the capital. It should be noted that the reverse design was revived in 1887 for use on the *East and West Africa Medal* and also used on the *East and Central Africa Medal* of 1891–98.

Top left: The reverse of the *Medal for the Abyssinia [Ethiopia] Campaign* of 1868. Both its obverse and reverse designs are highly unusual for its day; the reverse bears the embossed details of each British recipient – a very expensive procedure. Those to Indians tend to be engraved.

Right: Reverse of the medal for the Ashanti campaign of 1873–74, with its single clasp *Coomassie*. Widely regarded as one of the finest designs on a British war medal in terms of its detail and workmanship, it was also used on the *Central Africa Medal* of 1891–98 and the *East and West Africa Medal* of 1888–1900.

The campaign against Afghanistan in 1878–80, the 2nd Afghan War, also produced two distinctive medals. Originally it had been intended not to produce a separate war medal for the campaign, which went very well in its early stages, but simply to award the existing 1854 *India General Service Medal* (see below) with clasps *Ali Musjid* or *Peiwar Kotal* for the actions that opened the way to a successful British invasion in November–December 1878. However, once the war escalated following the British occupation of Kabul, the murder of the British resident and a general Afghan uprising, it was decided that an entirely new medal was appropriate. The *Afghan War Medal* of 1878–80 eventually bore six clasps, commemorating the major battles of what turned out to be a difficult campaign. *Kabul* rewarded a series of operations under Sir Fred Roberts around the capital city in December 1879, including the defence of the British base at Sherpur. *Kandahar* commemorated the last great battle of the war on 1 September 1880, in which General Roberts defeated the Afghans under Ayub Khan. The most famous – or infamous – incident in the war was the disastrous battle of Maiwand on 27 July 1880, where a British-Indian force from the Kandahar garrison was seriously defeated and suffered over 1,100 casualties. Medals to men who were present at Maiwand, especially in the 66th (Berkshire) Regiment or in 'E' Battery, 'B' Brigade, Royal Horse Artillery, are specially sought-after.

The need to relieve the besieged city of Kandahar following the defeat at Maiwand led to the dispatch from Kabul of a relief column under Sir Fred Roberts. The epic 'Kabul–Kandahar march' was one of the most famous military events of its day, with Roberts leading a 'strike force' of 10,000 men at great speed over rugged and dangerous country before decisively defeating the Afghan army outside Kandahar on 1 September 1880. Those who took part in the march were rewarded with a distinctive *Kabul to Kandahar Star*. Interestingly, it was made from enemy guns captured during the battle of Kandahar. Its attractive multi-coloured ribbon revived the one nicknamed 'sunrise in the east' used on the early Indian medals –

Above: The medal for the 2nd Afghan War, 1878–80; reverse, showing a British-Indian column on the march through mountainous terrain. Four of its associated battle clasps are seen here.

Afghanistan 1840–42, Gwalior 1843 and *Scinde*. Men who were given this Star were also, of course, recipients of the Afghan campaign medal, usually at least with clasp *Kandahar*, so received two awards.

The British invasion of Egypt in 1882 (largely to protect the Suez Canal and Britain's vital trade route to the east) resulted in the award to British, Indian and naval forces of the attractive *Egypt Medal* in 1882. Featuring on the reverse a solid depiction of the Sphinx over the date '1882', it was awarded with two clasps. *Alexandria 11th July* rewarded naval forces that had taken part in the bombardment of the port prior to a more serious British commitment on land in August. The one battle clasp was *Tel-el-Kebir*, awarded to those who served under Sir Garnet Wolseley in his remarkably successful advance on the Egyptian army position at Tel-el-Kebir which was stormed on 13th September 1882 following an overnight march. The medal ribbon's blue and white stripes are said to symbolise the Blue and White Niles.

This complete victory led to the British occupation of Cairo and, ultimately, to a more permanent British involvement in Egyptian affairs. Once in control of Egypt – and having destroyed her army – Britain was reluctantly pitched into the affairs of Egypt's southern province, the Sudan. Here, a fundamentalist Muslim movement led by Mohammed Ahmed, known as the Mahdi, was sweeping northwards. Since this posed a threat to Egyptian security (and therefore to the trade routes via the Suez Canal) British forces were called into action. The *Egypt Medal* was reissued but without date, with no clasp (largely to naval forces in Egyptian waters or troops serving on the frontier around Wadi Halfa) or with a range of clasps for subsequent campaigns in the Sudan. These were principally around the Red Sea port of

Top right: 51 *The Kabul to Kandahar Star* 1880. The reverse is plain but bears the details of the recipient.

Left: The dated *Egypt Medal* (1882) with five battle clasps, covering service in the British conquest of Egypt in 1882 (*Tel-el-Kebir*) and later in the Sudan, 1884–5. The recipient would have seen a lot of hard fighting, not least at Abu Klea.

Suakin in 1884 and 1885, where British, Indian and naval forces were deployed, and, most famously, along the Nile in 1884–85 for the attempted relief of General Gordon in Khartoum. Some hard-fought actions were commemorated by the different clasps, especially *El Teb* (29 February 1884), *Tamaai* (13 March 1884) and *Tofrek* (22 March 1885), all near Suakin. In these actions, the Sudanese tribesmen proved themselves to be formidable foes.

The clasp *The Nile 1884–85* was granted to the small force under General Wolseley that belatedly attempted the relief of Khartoum, where General Charles Gordon had been besieged by Mahdist forces since January 1884. Apart from a few full regiments, the Nile force comprised a mixture of units (infantry, cavalry and a naval brigade), the men selected as being the fittest or the best shots in their regiment. Many of the cavalry ended up on camels forming the novel Heavy or Light Cavalry Camel Corps. However, perhaps the most unusual feature of the campaign was the employment of 400 specially hired Canadian boatmen to man the vessels that took the troops and stores on their long journey southwards. Equally novel was the deployment at Suakin in 1885 of a force of infantry, medical personnel and artillery from New South Wales – the first occasion on which colonial troops served alongside British forces on an imperial campaign. Medals to these Canadian and Australian recipients are rare and highly collected, as are those of the small naval and Royal Marine brigade that was present in the campaign, but any medal to one of the soldiers engaged in this desperate adventure was well earned.

Two actions were fought by Wolseley's column. The clasp *Abu Klea* (17th January 1885) commemorated the ferocious action fought by the small Desert Column, sent ahead of the main force across the Bayuda Desert to reach Gordon's gunboats on the Nile and, hopefully, race on to relieve Khartoum. The battle was one of the most severe fought by British soldiers in the nineteenth century; out of only 1,600 men engaged, there were 400 casualties. Wolseley's main column, labouring southwards along the Nile itself, fought the battle of *Kirbekan* on 10th February 1885. However, as is well known, Khartoum fell before Wolseley's force could reach the city. With Gordon dead the whole campaign was called off and the battle-scarred Nile column eventually laboured its way back through the desert to Egypt.

Since the *Egypt Medal* was re-issued in essentially the same form and with the same ribbon for several campaigns (1882, 1884, 1884–86, 1888–89) and recipients only received one medal with appropriate clasps for later service, it could be regarded as a form of 'general service medal' (see below) for Egypt and the Sudan prior to 1896.

As Britain was technically acting on behalf of Egypt, all British and imperial forces (Indian, Australian and Canadian) received an award from the Khedive, the ruler of Egypt. Known as the *Khedive's Stars*, these heavy bronze awards bear various dates, according to the campaign commemorated – *1882* or *1884* or *1884–86*. An undated type was awarded for later actions in 1888–89, for which the British medal was given with clasps *Gemaizah 1888* (20th December 1888) and/or *Toski 1889* (3rd August 1889); comparatively few British forces were engaged in these later campaigns since by then Britain had reformed the Egyptian army and raised Sudanese regiments which were generally employed after 1886. Only one clasp was awarded with the *Khedive's Star*; *Tokar* was given to those engaged in the battle of 19th February 1891. The Star with this clasp is, incidentally, the only time that the Star could be worn without a British Egypt medal since the British award was not conferred for this action. It was mainly granted to Egyptian and Sudanese soldiers under British officers, though some men of the warships HMS *Sandfly* and *Dolphin* were present and received the Khedive's award.

It should be noted that recipients could receive and wear only one *Khedive's Star* – that for the first campaign in which they served – even if they subsequently took park in later expeditions for which Stars were awarded.

After the withdrawal from the Sudan, British forces and their Egyptian and Sudanese counterparts restricted their military activity to the defence of the Egyptian Frontier around Hadi Halfa. Not until 1896, in the face of the perceived threat of French and Italian intervention in the upper Nile region was further military action begun. In June 1896, British, Sudanese and Egyptian forces began the 'Dongola campaign', which marked the beginning of the Anglo-Egyptian reconquest of

Top right: An example of the bronze *Khedive's Star*. This one is dated '1882', for the British conquest of Egypt. Most were made by Messrs Jenkins of Birmingham and some have the maker's details on the reverse. Otherwise, the reverse is plain except for the crowned 'TM' cypher of Khedive Tewfik and is sometimes found privately engraved with the recipient's details.

Left: The silver medal for the Anglo-Egyptian reconquest of the Sudan, 1896–98. Unusually for its time, no clasps were awarded. The reverse (seen here) is another that is highly regarded for its artistic qualities.

the Sudan. This long and arduous campaign, fought under Herbert Kitchener, soon to become Lord Kitchener of Khartoum, effectively ended with the battle of Omdurman on 2nd September 1898 and the occupation of Khartoum. 'Mopping up' operations continued further into the depths of the Sudan beyond 1899.

British forces (and Indian soldiers based at Suakin) received a silver medal for service in the campaign of 1896–98. Regarded as one of the most attractive of British medallic designs, its obverse bears a seated Victory proffering palm and laurel branches. Unusually for Victorian awards, no clasps were awarded. However, as with the Khedive's awards for the 1882 and 1884–86 campaigns, a separate medal was awarded by the Khedive. A heavy and handsome award, the silver *Khedive's Sudan Medal* (1896–1908) bore a range of clasps, fifteen in all, inscribed in both English and Arabic, commemorating the major victories and advances of the campaign. Most British soldiers received only *Atbara*, for the battle of 8 April 1898, and/or *Khartoum*, for the battle of Omdurman (2nd September 1898) – a rare example of a clasp bearing the name other than that for the battle it commemorates. The most sought-after are medals to men of the 21st Lancers, famous for their dramatic charge at Omdurman, in which Winston Churchill participated. He was also its last-known survivor (d. 1965). Relatively few British soldiers received the other clasps, since few were engaged; some, however, received the early clasps *Firket* (7th June 1896) and/or *Hafir* (19th–20th September 1896). Very few medals were awarded to Royal Navy or Royal Marine personnel – mainly for manning the Nile gunboats that played a prominent part during the advance and in some actions, shelling enemy formations – so they are rarely seen and are valuable.

The other clasps on the 1896 *Khedive's Sudan Medal* (and the sixteen on its successor, the *Khedive's Sudan Medal 1910–22*) commemorate service in small-scale punitive expeditions in some of the most difficult and inhospitable parts of the Sudan. Few British personnel were involved, apart from officers, and most were awarded to Egyptian or Sudanese regiments. An exception is the *Khedive's Sudan Medal 1910–22* with clasp *Darfur 1916*, which was actually awarded to a number of British support personnel,

Above: The silver *Khedive's Sudan Medal* for the campaign of 1896–98, with clasp for the battle of the Atbara. The clasps are named in both English and Arabic.

mainly of the Army Service Corps and Royal Flying Corps. Some of these troops also qualified for the clasp *Fasher*.

The final major war of Victoria's campaign – she died while it was still in progress – was that fought against the Boers of the Transvaal and Orange Free State. What was known as the 'South African War', the '2nd Boer War' or the 'Transvaal War' produced a range of medals. The standard award to British and imperial forces (since Canadian, Australian, New Zealand and other colonial forces were employed) was *The Queen's South Africa Medal* (QSA). The war eventually involved some 400,000 imperial troops from all over the Empire and was a long and difficult affair, since the Boers proved to be skilful and elusive foes. The authorities really went to town on the issuing of clasps to the QSA (as opposed to battle honours, which were few). No fewer than twenty-six separate clasps could be earned and five or six to one recipient is not rare; nine is the maximum, but only a handful was awarded. They can be found to a wide range of units, which makes the medal an attractive proposition for the collector, ranging from the usual British infantry, cavalry, artillery and engineer units, to colonial volunteers from South Africa and all over the Empire, to naval and marine forces, civilian nurses and surgeons, British volunteer units and Imperial Yeomanry, local 'town guards' and scratch units raised on the spot especially for the war.

The rarest clasps are *Defence of Mafeking*, for the famous siege under Colonel Robert Baden-Powell, who later founded the Boy Scout movement, *Wepener*, for a lesser known siege and *Rhodesia* for operations within and across the Rhodesian Frontier. There were some famous 'disasters' during the war, embarrassing defeats for an imperial power, such as Colenso and Magersfontein in December 1899, which are not, of course, commemorated. Some of the clasps celebrate significant victories, examples being *Elaandslagte* (21 October 1899), *Belmont* (23rd November 1899), *Modder River* (28th November 1899), *Paardeburg* (17th–26th February 1900) – where a

Above: The *Queen's South Africa Medal* with seven battle clasps. The detailed reverse shows Britannia holding a laurel wreath above her forces – infantry, cavalry and navy.

whole Boer army surrendered – *Driefontein* (10th March 1900) and *Diamond Hill* (11th–12th June 1900). Others commemorate the famous sieges and reliefs of the war – *Defence of Mafeking* (13th October 1899–17th May 1900), *Defence of Ladysmith* (3rd November 1899–28th February 1900), *Defence of Kimberley*(15th October 1899–15th February 1900) – the diamond centre and residence of Cecil Rhodes – and the associated relief of those towns, *Relief of Mafeking*(17th May 1900), *Relief of Ladysmith* (15th December 1899–28th February 1900) and *Relief of Kimberley* (15th February 1900).

Some clasps represent a series of operations, as with *Tugela Heights* (14th–27th February 1900), for General Buller's costly attacks across the Tugela in an attempt to break the siege of Ladysmith, and *Wittebergen*, for the pursuit campaigns along the Basutoland border against the highly mobile commandos of Christian de Wet in July 1900. Many recipients who had not been present in any particular action or had spent some time in one area received area clasps – *Cape Colony, Orange Free State, Transvaal, Natal* or *Rhodesia*; some who received simply these clasps may nevertheless have seen considerable action. Medals without clasps were awarded to civilian nurses and doctors, naval personnel who did not land or receive any of the land clasps and those guarding Boer prisoners overseas (e.g. on St Helena). There were two dated clasps – *South Africa 1901* and *South Africa 1902* – also awarded, largely to those serving in the later, smaller operations that often involved long pursuits but which did not lead to large-scale battles worthy of commemoration with a special clasp. Bronze medals without clasp were awarded to non-combatants, mainly servants, medical orderlies and remount staff from Indian units. No regular Indian forces were deployed in the active operations, but some served in remount, transport and medical units, mostly receiving the bronze version of the medal.

As originally conceived, the medal was to bear on the reverse the dates '1899–1900', in the expectation that the war would end once the Boer capitals Pretoria and Johannesburg had been captured in 1900. As is well known, the Boers did not surrender and the war dragged on into a 'guerrilla' phase until May 1902. As a result, few of the medals with dated reverse were ever issued, so that examples are very rare, but one sometimes sees 'ghost dates' lingering on the reverse after the erasure of the original dates from the dies.

Since the Queen died in January 1901 while the war was still in progress and was succeeded by Edward VII, a second medal, *The King's South Africa* (KSA) was introduced. It was not awarded by itself – recipients had to have qualified for the QSA – and in stark contrast to the QSA bore only two clasps, *South Africa 1901* and *South Africa 1902*, once more reflecting the fact that the campaign had moved away from large set-piece battles. The

The obverses of the *Queen's South Africa Medal*, paired with the *King's South Africa Medal*. The reverses of these awards for the Boer War of 1899–1902 are essentially the same (see p. 43). Only two 'general' dated clasps were awarded with the KSA.

KSA is rare to the Imperial Yeomanry (most of whom had returned to Britain by 1901) and to naval forces, since most were no longer serving ashore. It was awarded without clasps to nurses and may be seen (in rare cases) with only one clasp, usually *South Africa 1902*, where a soldier had broken service and later returned to South Africa.

Apart from these official awards, some unofficial and local medals were produced. The best known is the relatively common *Mayor's Siege Medal* for the defence of Kimberley – a hallmarked silver star produced by the city's Mayor and awarded to those who served in the defence. A rarer example is Cape Copper Company's bronze medal for the *Defence of O'okiep*. Many British towns and cities also produced their own 'tribute medals' (now highly collected) to give to local men, often from volunteer and yeomanry units, as a token of regard from the local community and a reward for their war service on their return. Most were produced in small numbers and are rare. (For a detailed study, see *Boer War Tribute Medals*, M G Hibbard, Constantia Classics, Sandton, South Africa, 1982.)

The twentieth century began not just with a major war in South Africa and a campaign in China ('the Boxer Rebellion' of 1900), but also with the continuation of small-scale expeditions in east and west Africa and two campaigns on opposite sides of the globe – the Ashanti uprising in 1900 and the larger Tibet campaign of 1903–4. The Ashanti uprising followed on the heels of the British annexation of the West African Ashanti kingdom in 1896, a bloodless campaign for which an unusual gun-metal star was awarded to approximately 2,200 participating troops (see photograph on p. 56). No British soldiers, apart from officers and few NCOs with local regiments, were involved in the Ashanti campaign in the Gold Coast in 1900. The attractive *Ashanti Medal* was mainly given to local West African forces and carried only one clasp, *Kumassi*, awarded for those who took part in the relief or defence of the capital during the rebellion, which saw some severe fighting. The Tibet campaign was very much the last throw of the dice in what has been called 'the great game' – the process of inter-imperial rivalry between Russian, Great Britain and China on the frontiers of India. In this case, it was fear of Chinese expansion towards India that precipitated the Younghusband Mission, a British-Indian expedition to Lhasa to force a treaty on the Dalai Lama. This campaign, waged at the highest altitude ever attempted by a military force, involved few British troops – part of the 1st Royal Fusiliers and some mountain artillery in the main. Most of the fighting force was Indian or Gurkha and there were literally tens of thousands of transport drivers, Indian and locally recruited (e.g. in Sikkim), working with the huge mule and yak columns that were needed to transport food and equipment at incredible heights and in the most intense cold. Only one clasp, *Gyantse*, was awarded, for the attack on Gyantse Jong (fort) in July 1904 and for the subsequent fighting around the town. The Tibetans on

Top left: The silver *Kimberley Star* or *Mayor's Siege Medal* (as on the otherwise plain reverse). Awarded by the Mayor for the defence of the diamond-mining town between 15 October 1899 and 15 February 1900. Most were awarded to the Town Guard and colonial units. As an unofficial award, it was not allowed to be worn in uniform by British soldiers.

Above right: An example of an unofficial medal for the Boer War. This one – to the 3rd (Yorkshire) Imperial Yeomanry and for 1900–1 – is one of three different types produced in silver by the Yorkshire IY. Made by Spink and Son.

occasion showed themselves to be determined opponents in the face of modern weapons, like machine-guns, but it was the cold, the long distances and the altitude that caused most of the problems. The British eventually forced their treaty on the Tibetans, but apart from small garrisons left near the Indian side of the frontier, really left Tibet in peace thereafter.

Principal British Medals and Clasps, 1840–1914

Medal rolls, where noted, are held at TNA (WO.100 series for Army personnel or ADM.171 series for naval recipients) or the India Office Collections in the British Library (L.Mil.5 series).

The St Jean d'Acre Medal, 1840

This award, conferred by the Sultan of Turkey, was actually the first official medal given to the Royal Navy and Marines after the unofficial types of the Napoleonic Wars and was issued in 1842 to Royal Navy and Royal Marine forces (and a few attached military personnel) that were present in operations in the Eastern Mediterranean and at the bombardment of Acre on 3 November 1840. Gold, silver and bronze versions were awarded, according to rank. Most of its recipients later received the *Naval General Service Medal* with clasp *Syria*.

The Scinde Campaign, 1843

A silver medal for Sir Charles Napier's campaign to subjugate the Scinde region on the North West Frontier of India in the wake of the 1st Afghan War and authorised in July 1843. (See photograph on p. 22.)

    Reverse: *Meeanee*
    Reverse: *Hyderabad*
    Reverse: *Meeanee-Hyderabad*
    Medal roll: L.Mil.5-69 (HMs 22nd Regt and EIC forces)

The Gwalior Star, 1843

The awards for the brief campaign to subjugate the state of Gwalior in 1843 took the form of a bronze star with a silver central inset naming one of two battles fought on the same day,

Above: Star for the Gwalior campaign, 1843. Made from captured guns, two types were awarded. One (seen here) has the centre for *Maharajpoor* and the other for *Punniar* – two decisive battles fought on the same day, 29 December 1843. The medal was originally – and uniquely – attached to the jacket pocket by a brass hook on the reverse but most (as here) were adapted to be worn like other medals.

29 December 1843. Authorised by the EIC in January 1844, they were made from the metal of enemy field guns captured during the campaign.

Centre: *Maharajpoor*
Centre: *Punniar*

No surviving medal rolls.

Medal for the 1st Sikh War: the Sutlej Campaign, 1845–46

A silver medal issued to British and EIC forces for the 1st Sikh War, 1846–48. The first action is named on the reverse of the medal, others are borne as clasps. Those who did not serve in any of the four selected battles received no medal. With clasp(s) or reverse inscription:.

Moodkee
Ferozeshuhur
Aliwal
Sobroan

Medal rolls: L.Mil.5-70 (British and EIC)

*   *The Army of the Sutlej 1845–46: Casualty Roll*, P Newman (with J B Hayward, n.p., *c.* 1986).

Medal for the 2nd Sikh War: the Punjab Campaign, 1848–49

A silver medal issued to British and EIC forces for the 2nd Sikh War, 1848–49. Some were awarded without clasp (e.g. to the Indus River flotilla) for service in the Punjab but not in the major battles (see photograph on p. 22). Clasps:

Mooltan
Chilianwala
Goojerat

Medal roll:

*   L.Mil.5-71 (British) and L.Mil.5-72 (East India Co. forces)
*   WO.100-13 (HMs 10th, 24th, 32nd and 61st Regiments only)
*   *The Punjab Campaign 1848–49: Casualty Roll* (London, London Stamp Exchange, *c.* 1986).

The Medal for the Baltic Campaign, 1854–55

This silver medal was awarded for the British and French naval campaign in the Baltic in 1854–55. No clasps and issued un-named, apart from those to the Sappers and Miners. (See photograph on p. 31.)

Medal rolls: ADM.171-19 to 221 (no Army rolls).

The Medal for the Crimean War, 1854–56

The silver medal awarded for the land campaign against Russia in 1854–56 and naval operations in the Black Sea and Sea of Azoff (see photograph on p. 32). Mostly awarded un-named, but some were officially impressed and many are found privately engraved. Some were issued without clasps, mainly to naval forces operating in the Black Sea. Clasps:

Alma
Balaklava
Inkermann
Azoff
Sebastopol

Medal rolls:

- WO.100-22, 23 (Royal Artillery and RE)
- WO.100-24 (Cavalry)
- WO.100- 25 (Guards)
- WO.100-26 to 33 (Infantry)
- WO.100-34 (Turkish and miscellaneous units)
- WO.100-364 (presentations by the Queen)
- ADM.171-23 and 24 (Navy: clasps *Sebastopol, Inkermann, Balaklava*)
- ADM.171-25 (Navy: *Azoff* clasp)
- *Casualty Roll for the Crimean War 1854–56*, F and A Cook (London, Hayward, 1978)
- *The Azoff campaign, 1855*, P Duckers and C N Mitchell (n.p., Squirrel, 1997): medal rolls and dispatches
- *Presented by the Queen: The Crimea Medal Award Ceremony 18th May 1855*, P Duckers and C N Mitchell (n.p., Jade, 1998): roll of recipients
- *Honour the Light Brigade*, W M Lummis and K G Wynn (London, Hayward, 1973)
- *Forgotten Heroes: the Charge of the Light Brigade*, R Dutton (n.p., Infodial, 2007).

The Turkish Medal for the Crimean War, 1854–56

Since Britain, France and (later) Sardinia were fighting in the Crimea in 1854–56 in defence of Ottoman Turkey, the Sultan awarded a silver medal to the military and naval forces of his allies. (See photograph on p. 33.)

British reverse: *Crimea 1855*
Sardinian reverse: *La Crimea 1855*
French reverse: *La Crimee 1855*

Medal rolls:
- WO.100-373
- ADM.171-26 to 28.

The Medal for the Indian Mutiny, 1857–59

The medal awarded for the arduous campaign for the suppression of 'the Indian Mutiny', 1857–59. (See photograph on p. 34.) Awarded without or without clasp. No bronze version. Clasps:
Delhi
Defence of Lucknow (original defenders and 1st relief force)
Relief of Lucknow
Lucknow
Central India

Medal rolls:
- WO.100-35 to 39: British regiments
- WO.100-405: 75th Regtiment
- ADM.171-29 (*Shannon* and *Pearl* Naval Brigades)
- L.Mil.5-71 to 76: British regiments and units
- L.Mil.5-77 to 80: Bengal army regiments
- L.Mil.5-77 to 82: Madras army regiments
- L.Mil.5-77 to 82: Bombay army regiments
- L.Mil.5-66 (naval personnel)
- L.Mil.5-85 (RN and RM)
- *Casualty Roll for the Indian Mutiny, 1857–59*, Ian Tavender (London, Hayward, 1983)
- *The Indian Mutiny: Alphabetical Roll: British Units*, K J Asplin (n.p., 1998).

The Medal for the 2nd China War, 1856–1860

A silver medal awarded for the two stages of the war, 1856–58 and 1860. Awarded un-named (and many without clasp) to naval forces; officially named to military units. (See photograph on p. 35.)

China 1842 (technically to be added to 1842 China medal, if already awarded).

Fatshan 1857
Canton 1857
Taku Forts 1858
Taku Forts 1860
Pekin 1860

Medal rolls:

- ADM.171-30 to 34
- L.Mil.5-66 (RN)
- L.Mil.5-106 (Indian Navy)
- *The China Medal Roll, 1856–60*, K J Asplin (London, Savannah, 2004).

The New Zealand Medal for the Maori Wars, 1845–47 and 1860–66

A silver medal without clasps awarded 1869–70 for service in the Maori Wars. Various dated reverses, reflecting when the recipient saw active service. (See photograph on p. 36.)

First War

undated	*1846*
1845–46	*1847*
1845–47	*1848*
1846–47	

Second War

undated	*1862–66*
1860	*1863*
1860–61	*1863–64*
1860–63	*1863–65*
1860–64	*1863–66*
1860–65	*1864*
1860–66	*1864–65*
1861	*1864–66*
1861–63	*1865*
1861–64	*1865–66*
1861–65	*1866*
1861–66	

Medal rolls:
- WO.100-18 and 19
- ADM.171-16 (for 1845–47 and 1866–70)
- *The New Zealand Medal to Colonials, 1845–72*, R Stowers (Hamilton NZ, 1999).

The Medal for the Abyssinian Campaign, 1867–68

A distinctive silver medal to British and Indian forces, military and naval, for service against King Theodore of Magdala. No clasps. (See photograph on p. 37.)

Medal rolls:
- WO.100-19 (Artillery) and WO.100-43 (rest)
- ADM.171-36.

The Medal for the Ashanti War, 1873–74

A silver medal for service with naval and Royal Marine forces or under Sir Garnet Wolseley against the Ashanti Empire of the Gold Coast (now Ghana), 1873–74. Awarded without clasp (e.g. to RN forces) or with *Coomassie* for the fighting at Amoaful and the occupation of the capital. (See photograph on p. 37.)

Medal rolls:
- WO.100-42 (Artillery) and WO.100-44 (others)
- ADM.171-37.

The Medal for the 2nd Afghan War, 1878–80

Silver and bronze medals (the latter very rare) were awarded with or without clasps to British and Indian units for service in Afghanistan. (See photograph on p. 38.)

Ali Musjid	*Kabul*
Peiwar Kotal	*Ahmed Khel*
Charasia	*Kandahar*

Medal rolls:
- WO.100-51 to 54 (British units)
- L.Mil.5-110 to 116 (British Army)
- L.Mil.5-117 to 120 (Bengal and Bombay armies)
- L.Mil.5-121 (Madras army)
- L.Mil.5-124 (Indian army in general)

- *The Second Afghan War 1878–80*, A Farrington (London, London Stamp Exchange, 1987): casualty roll and some dispatches.

The Kabul to Kandahar Star, 1880

A bronze star made from guns captured at the battle of Kandahar on 1st September 1880 and commemorating Sir Fred Roberts' 'Kabul to Kandahar' march and the battle of Kandahar. It is suspended from the old 'sunrise in the east' or 'India ribbon' previously used on Indian campaign medals of 1842–43. No clasps awarded. (See photograph on p. 39.)

Medal rolls:

- L.Mil.5-112 (British units)
- L.Mil.5-12 and 124 (Indian units).

The Medal for Egypt and the Sudan, 1882–1889

The silver medal awarded for the conquest of Egypt in 1882 (with that date on the reverse) or for subsequent operations in the Eastern Sudan and along the Nile, 1884–85 and 1888–89 (without date). (See photograph on p. 39.)

Alexandria 11th July
Tel-el-Kebir
El Teb
Tamaai
El Teb – Tamaai
Suakin 1884
The Nile 1884–85
Abu Klea (not awarded singly: with *The Nile 1884–85*)
Kirbekan (not awarded singly: with *The Nile 1884–85*)
Tofrek (not awarded singly: with *Suakin 1885*)
Gemaizah
Toski 1889

Medal rolls:

- 1882: WO.100-42 (Artillery); WO.100-54 to 61 (rest)
- 1884–91: WO.100-42 (Artillery); WO.100-62 to 68 (rest)
- ADM.171-41 (1882) and ADM.171-42 and 43 (1884–85)
- *Egypt 1882: Dispatches, Casualties, Awards*, P Duckers (London, Spink, 2001)
- *The Abu Klea Medal Rolls*, J V Webb (privately published, 1981).

The Khedive's Bronze Stars for Egypt and the Sudan, 1882–91

Dated bronze stars awarded by the Khedive of Egypt to British, Indian, Egyptian and Sudanese troops who took part in the 1882–89 campaigns or at Tokar, 1891. Recipients of any Egypt medal were automatically entitled to one of these awards, with appropriate date of their first campaign. (See photograph on p. 41.)

Dated '1882'
Dated '1884'
Dated '1884–86'
Undated
Undated, with *Tokar* clasp.

Medal rolls: entitlement noted by 'S' or 'Star' (usually with date of dispatch) on Egypt medal rolls.

- ADM.171-50 (1891 campaign and *Tokar* clasp).

The Medal for North West Canada, 1885

The silver medal for service in the second Louis Riel rebellion in 1885, mainly given to local Canadian forces. One clasp, *Saskatchewan*, was issued but most awarded without clasp. Very few British troops were involved.

- *North West Canada Medal Roll (Riel Rebellion 1885)*, Pacific Publication Co. (eds) (n.p., 1975).

The Royal Niger Company Medal for West Africa, 1886–99

Authorised in 1899 and granted to Royal Niger Company forces who served in a variety of punitive or expansionist campaigns between 1886–97. Bronze awards to African recipients are usually just numbered and not named. Not awarded without clasp.

Silver with bar *Nigeria 1886–97* to Europeans.
Bronze with bar *Nigeria* to African Other Ranks.

The Imperial British East Africa Company's Medal, 1890

Like the Royal Niger Company's medal, this was awarded to the forces of a Chartered Company given rights of exploration and administration, in this case Sir Charles McKinnon's British East Africa Company. Only a few Europeans received this silver medal, which is very rare.

The British South Africa Company Medal, 1890–97

This was another campaign medal awarded by a Chartered Company (the BSAC of Cecil Rhodes) for issue to its own and associated forces for campaigns in its sphere of influence. Issued in silver, with or without clasp, the first campaign being named on the medal's reverse. Very few British troops were involved. Reverse or clasp:

Mashonaland 1890
Matabeleland 1893
Rhodesia 1896
Mashonaland 1897

Medal rolls:

- WO.100-42 and WO.100-77

- *The British South Africa Company Medal Roll, 1878–1893–1896–97*, D R Forsyth (Johannesburg, 1980)

- *The British South Africa Company Medal Roll, 1890–97*, C R Owen (n.p., n.d.)

- *The British South Africa Company Medal Rolls, 1890–97* (n.p., Roberts Publications, 1993).

The Medal for Campaigns in Central Africa, 1891–98

A silver medal (also known in bronze) authorised in 1895, this rewarded service in small-scale tribal expeditions in the area around the East African great lakes and in what became Uganda between 1891 and 1898. Issued without clasp (from a ring suspension) for service 1891–94 or with clasp *Central Africa 1894–8* (and altered suspension). Usually seen to Indian and African soldiers; rare to British recipients.

Top : An example of a Chartered Company's award: the British South Africa Company's Medal for Cecil Rhodes' campaigns of 1890–97. Reverse for *Matabeleland 1893* and additional clasps for *Rhodesia 1896* and *Mashonaland 1897*. The Royal Niger Company and Imperial British East Africa Company also awarded their own medals.

Right: The medal for *Central Africa 1891–98*, with clasp for the campaigns of 1894–98, and the *India General Service Medal, 1908–35*, with its first awarded clasp for the North West Frontier operations of 1908. These obverses show the later 'veiled head' of Queen Victoria and the effigy of Edward VII in Field Marshal's uniform.

Medal rolls:
- WO.100-42: Royal Artillery
- WO.100-76: recipients from a scattering of British units and Indian recipients from various regiments of the Indian army.

The Ashanti Star, 1896

An unusual gun-metal star awarded to the approximately 2,200 men comprising General Francis Scott's expeditionary force to Kumassi on the Gold Coast (now Ghana) to depose King Prempeh and annex the Ashanti kingdom.

Medal rolls:
- WO.100-42 (Artillery)
- WO.100-79 (rest)
- *Ashanti 1895–96*, I McInnes and M Fraser (Picton, 1987): rolls and campaign details.

The Queen's Medal for the Sudan Campaign, 1896–98

Issued in 1899, this silver medal was the standard award for the Anglo-Egyptian re-conquest of the Sudan between 1896–99 and was given to British, Indian, Egyptian and Sudanese units, and these also received the *Khedive's Sudan Medal* with appropriate clasp(s). It was issued in bronze to Indian 'followers' and non-combatants. No clasps issued. (See photograph on p. 41.)

Medal rolls:
- WO.100-42 (Royal Artillery)
- WO.100-80 and 81 (RN, RM with British Army rolls)
- WO.100-82 (Indian army and miscellaneous).

The Khedive of Egypt's Medal for Campaigns in the Sudan, 1896–1908

Instituted in February 1897 by Khedive Abbas Hilmi and granted to British, Indian, Egyptian and Sudanese forces who served in the re-conquest of 1896–98 and to the largely Egyptian and Sudanese forces who served

Above: The Star awarded for the bloodless Ashanti campaign of 1896, which led to the deposition of King Prempeh and the annexation of the Ashanti Empire to the Gold Coast. Issued unnamed, the reverse simply has 'From the Queen'.

between 1898–1908 in further operations and punitive expeditions. Awarded without clasp (e.g. for service at Suakin on the Red Sea in 1896) and also in bronze. (See photograph on p. 42.)

Firket	*Nyima*
Hafir	*Gedid*
Abu Hamed	*Sudan 1899*
Sudan 1897	*Bahr-el Ghazal 1900–2*
The Atbara	*Jerok*
Khartoum	*Nyam-Nyam*
Katfia	*Talodi*
Gedaref	

Medal rolls:

- WO.100-406 (*Talodi, Nyima, Katfia* only)

- ADM.171-51 (not all clasps listed).

The Medal for Campaigns in East and Central Africa, 1897–99

Awarded for a series of campaigns largely caused by mutinous Sudanese troops in the Southern Sudan or for punitive expeditions in Uganda. Issued in silver and bronze versions, the latter rare.

No clasp
Lubwa's (always with *Uganda 1897–98*)
Uganda 1897–98
1898
Uganda 1899

Medal rolls:

- WO.100-90: mainly to Indian and African recipients; few British recipients.

The British North Borneo Company's Medals, 1897–1916

Another medal issued by a private company, the British North Borneo Company, and given for fifteen small punitive expeditions in Brunei, Sabah and Borneo between 1883 and 1916. Never issued without a clasp, it was also awarded in bronze. A rare medal.

Above: The *East and Central Africa Medal*, 1896–99, with two clasps. The reverse design – Britannia offering peace and law as a new dawn rises over Africa – was also used on the *Africa General Service Medal* (1902–56).

Punitive Expedition
Punitive Expeditions
Rundum

The Queen's South Africa Medal, 1899–1902

The first medal issued for the protracted South African or Boer War of 1899–1902, with no fewer than twenty-six separate clasps. Awarded with or without clasps and in bronze (largely to Indian 'followers') without clasp. (See photographs on pp. 43 and 45.)

No clasp	*Orange Free State*
Cape Colony	*Relief of Ladysmith*
Rhodesia	*Driefontien*
Relief of Mafeking	*Wepener*
Defence of Kimberley	*Defence of Mafeking*
Talana	*Transvaal*
Elandslaagte	*Johannesberg*
Defence of Ladysmith	*Laing's Nek*
Belmont	*Diamond Hill*
Modder River	*Wittebergen*
Tugela Heights (not awarded as a single clasp)	*Belfast*
Natal	*South Africa 1901*
Relief of Kimberley	*South Africa 1902*
Paardeberg	

Medal rolls:

- WO.100-112 to 119 (Cavalry)
- WO.100-120 to 136 (Imperial Yeomanry)
- WO.100-139 to 154 (Royal Artillery)
- WO.100-155 to 162 (Royal Engineers)
- WO.100-163 to 211 (Infantry)
- WO.100-212 to 235 (Corps, Medical, Chaplains)
- WO.100-236 to 295 (Colonial and Overseas units)
- WO.100-296 to 298 (miscellaneous Indian units)
- ADM.171-53 and 54.

The King's South Africa Medal, 1901–2

Since Queen Victoria died in January 1901 while the South African War was still in progress, a second silver medal for the campaign was issued, the obverse of which bore the effigy and titles of the new king Edward VII. It was never issued by itself, but should always be seen with the *Queen's South Africa Medal*. Awards to the Royal Navy and Imperial Yeomanry are rare. No bronze versions were awarded. (See photograph on p. 45.)

South Africa 1901
South Africa 1902

Medal rolls:

- WO.100-302 to 305 (Cavalry)
- WO.100-306 to 312 (Royal Artillery)
- WO.100-313 to 316 (Royal Engineers)
- WO.100-317 to 348 (Infantry)
- WO.100-349 to 352 (Corps: ASC, RA, AOC etc.)
- WO.100-353 to 357 (miscellaneous: Nurses, Yeomanry etc.)
- WO.100-358 to 370 (Colonial and Overseas units)
- ADM.171-53 and 54
- *The Queen's South Africa Medal to the Royal Navy and Royal Marines*, W H Fevyer and J W Wilson (London, Spink, 1983)
- *Afloat and Ashore: the Royal Navy during the Boer War 1899–1902*, P Singlehurst (Honiton, Token, 2006)
- *The South African Field Force Casualty Roll, 1899–1902* (London, Hayward, 1976)
- *The Natal Field Force Casualty Roll* (London, Hayward, 1980)
- *Elandslaagte: Account and Medal Roll*, D Biggins (Honiton, Token, 2004)
- *The Last Post: Officers who gave their lives in the South African War 1899–1900*, M G Dooner (n.p., 1990)
- *The Boer War Casualty List*, A Palmer (Perth, AUS, A Palmer, 1999).

The Mediterranean Medal, 1899–1902

Awarded to volunteers from the Militia who served in Britain's Mediterranean garrisons in Gibraltar, Malta and Cyprus to free Regular troops for service in South Africa. No clasps. No bronze versions were awarded. Essentially the same as the QSA but with '*Mediterranean*' in place of '*South Africa*' on the reverse.

Medal rolls:

- WO.100-368.

The Star for the Defence of Kimberley, 1899–1900

An 'unofficial' award, the hallmarked silver star was conferred by the Mayor of Kimberley for the defence of the town. It accompanies the *Queen's South Africa Medal* with clasp *Defence of Kimberley*. (See photograph on p. 46.)

The Medal for the China War, 1900

The last British medal for an actual campaign in China was awarded for the 'Boxer Rebellion' of 1900. Its most famous feature was siege of the Legations (embassies) in Peking and their relief by an international force. The medal is essentially the same as that awarded for earlier China Wars, but with the date '1900' added to the reverse. Issued with or without clasp and in bronze to Indian non-combatants.

No clasp
Taku Forts
Defence of Legations
Relief of Pekin

Medal rolls:

- WO.100-94 to 96 (British Army)
- WO.100-97 (Chinese and miscellaneous)
- WO.100-98 and 99 (Indian army)
- ADM.171-55
- *The China War Medal 1900 to the Royal Navy and Royal Marines*, W H Fevyer and J W Wilson (London, Spink, 1985).

The Transport Medal, 1899–1902

An unusual award intended only for Masters and senior officers of merchant vessels serving in military operations. It was presumably meant to continue in use after 1902 but was not awarded after that date. Issued in silver; never awarded without clasp (and sometimes with both).

S. Africa 1899–1902
China 1900

Medal rolls:

- ADM.171-52.

The *Transport Medal*, with clasp *South Africa 1899–1902*. Awarded only to the officers of merchant ships and troop ships serving in support of the operations in South Africa during the Boer War. Another clasp was awarded for similar duties during the 'Boxer Rebellion' in China in 1900.

The Medal for the Ashanti War, 1900

Sanctioned in October 1900, the last medal for campaigns against the Ashanti was awarded for the uprising of 31 March–25 December 1900, which involved the siege and relief of the capital, Kumassi, as well as operations in the surrounding country. Awarded in silver and bronze (rare), with or without the single clasp *Kumassi*.

Medal roll:

- WO.100-93.

The Medal for the Tibet Campaign, 1903–4

Authorised on 1 February 1905 for British and Indian forces and to local levies and porters who served beyond the frontier town of Siligari in the expedition to Tibet under Sir Francis Younghusband between 13 December 1903 and 23 September 1904. Awarded in silver and bronze, with or without its single clasp *Gyantse*. Very common in bronze, since thousands were issued to the civilian drivers of yak and mule teams etc.

Medal roll:

- WO.100-395: *British* recipients in British and Indian forces
- *The Royal Fusiliers: Tibet 1904*, J P Kelleher (n.p., Roberts Publications, 1995): annotated roll, also available on CD ROM from Royal Fusiliers museum.

The Medal for the Zulu Rebellion in Natal, 1906

Awarded only to local Natal units for service in a rebellion in Zululand in 1906. Issued only in silver, with or without dated clasp '1906'. Unusually, it is rarer *without* clasp.

- *The Natal Native Rebellion 1906: Medal Roll*, D R Forsyth (privately published, 1976)
- *The Natal Zulu Rebellion, 1906*, Roberts Publications (n.p., n.d.).

The Khedive's Medal for Campaigns in the Sudan, 1910–25

This medal replaced the *Khedive's Sudan Medal* of 1896–1908 and was awarded largely to Egyptian and Sudanese regiments, under British officers and some NCOs, for service in campaigns in the Sudan. Awarded in silver and bronze, with or without clasp.

Atwot
S. Kordofan 1910
Sudan 1912
Zeraf 1913–14
Mandal
Miri
Mongalla 1915–16
Darfur 1916

Fasher
Lau Nuer
Nyima 1917–18
Atwot 1918
Garjak Nuer
Aliab Dinka
Nyala
Darfur 1921

Medal roll:

* WO.100-407.

The *Khedive's Sudan Medal*, 1910–22; reverse (designed by Richard Garve) with clasp *Zeraf 1913–14*. Awarded for punitive expeditions in the Sudan, few British troops received these medals. The obverse bore the Arabic titles and cypher, amended in 1918, of Khedive Abbas Hilmi II.

Chapter Six

THE INTRODUCTION OF
GENERAL SERVICE MEDALS

While the larger wars of the nineteenth century – like the Crimean War, the Indian Mutiny, the Abyssinian campaign of 1868, the Afghan War 1878–80 and others – continued to be rewarded with separate campaign medals, often with distinctive battle clasps, it became clear as early as the 1850s that there was a risk of simply awarding too many medals. This became all the more apparent with the plethora of small-scale colonial campaigns, 'punitive expeditions' and the like which characterised the defence of Britain's imperial frontiers and the great expansion of Britain's tropical Empire after 1880. Giving each small-scale frontier campaign its own distinctive award would have been out of the question.

Thus was born the idea of the 'general service' medal. This would be an award dedicated to one region – like India, Egypt and the Sudan, South Africa, West Africa etc. – where entitled personnel would receive an initial medal and named or dated clasp but subsequent service in the same area would be rewarded simply with an extra clasp or clasps added to the existing medal and denoting service in that campaign at that time. The result was that soldiers who frequently saw active service in one geographical or colonial area – like the North West Frontier of India – would receive just one medal, but it might in the end carry a multiplicity of clasps covering a number of separate small-scale campaigns over a wide range of time.

Perhaps the first real 'general service' award was that for South Africa. The *South Africa Medal*, instituted in 1853, and bearing that date, rewarded service in any of three campaigns (the sixth, seventh and eighth 'frontier wars') which marked the expansion of British influence over the hinterland of the Cape Colony. These campaigns were fought in 1834–55, 1846–47 and 1850–53 against major local tribes. The medals were granted retrospectively to British, naval and colonial units but there is no difference in the design or ribbon for any of the three campaigns and no clasps were issued; only an examination of the medal rolls will confirm which campaign (or campaigns)

the recipient served in. The medal design and ribbon were re-issued to cover South African campaigns in the period 1877–79, the only design difference being the replacement of the reverse date '1853' with a shield and crossed spears. For these later campaigns against the Gaika, Griqua, Basuto and Zulu, waged by British regular regiments and a fascinating multiplicity of locally raised colonial units, the medal was issued with dated clasps. The seven clasps issued were *1877, 1877–78, 1878, 1878–79, 1877–79, 1877-8-9* and *1879*. The rarest is *1877–79*, with fewer than a dozen known awards; another is *1877*, of which only approximately 150 were issued, since many men (mainly in colonial units) served in other years and received other dates on their clasp. It should be noted that the clasps reflect service in the years shown in 1877 *and* 1879 (e.g. not throughout the whole period). Medals were awarded to naval forces with clasps for those who landed and took part in land operations or without clasps, to those engaged in support operations offshore (e.g. landing troops and supplies). Some clasps are rare to naval personnel since few were involved ashore (e.g. *1878* awarded to only seventy-five men of HMS *Active*).

The most famous of the campaigns – and probably the most written-about British imperial campaign of the nineteenth century – was that waged against the Zulu between January and July 1879. It involved the famous defeat and massacre at Isandhlwana on 22 January 1879 (where the 24th Regiment (2nd Warwickshire) was particularly badly hit, with 600 killed out of a casualty list of over 1,300 British dead) and the epic defence of Rorke's Drift on the 22–23 January. The defence of this mission station, again largely in the hands of the 24th Foot and a few 'odd' men who were in the hospital, saw the award of no fewer than eleven Victoria Crosses. Needless to say, medals to men who were at Isandhlwana or Rorke's Drift are highly sought-after and very expensive, as are gallantry awards for the campaign. Most of the medals for the Zulu campaign bore the clasp *1879* but some carry *1878–79* or *1877-8-9* (for regiments like the 13th, 24th or 90th

Above: The obverse and reverse of the *South Africa Medal* 1877–79, showing the clasp 1877-8-9 for campaign service in each of those years.

which had already served in previous frontier wars and went on to serve against the Zulu).

The first of the major 'area' awards was the *India General Service Medal 1854* (IGS), which remained current until 1895. Made retrospective to cover operations on the North West Frontier since 1849 and the Pegu campaign in Burma in 1852, it eventually had twenty-four separate clasps covering service in 'small wars' on the Indian frontiers (east and west) or within the orbit of the Indian Empire, like *Persia* in 1857 or *Perak* in 1874. The clasp *North West Frontier* was awarded for no fewer than sixteen separate frontier campaigns between 1849 and 1868, i.e. nearly twenty years covered by one clasp – a situation not repeated until the use of the *Northern Ireland* clasp over a hundred yearslater. Only an examination of the medalroll will clarify which campaign or campaigns the recipient served in. Some of the clasps eventually awarded were rare because of the small numbers engaged or the brief period of the campaign – like *Hunza 1891*, *Chin Hills 1892–93* and *Kachin Hills 1892–93*. Most British soldiers received only one or two clasps (most commonly for the conquest of Upper Burma, 1885–89) but some Indian recipients, especially those in units that were frequently deployed on India's frontiers, like the Gurkhas and units of the Punjab Frontier Force, might ultimately receive five, six or seven clasps. In the end, this was seen to devalue the medal as an adequate reward for years of hard service, since a soldier serving in, say, six campaigns over twenty years would wear only one medal.

The result was the decision in 1895 to introduce a new IGS, the *India General Service Medal 1895*. Prior to its replacement in 1908, this carried only seven clasps, the rarest being *Defence of Chitral* (1895), largely awarded to Kashmiri troops and some Sikhs, and the most common being *Punjab Frontier 1897–98* and *Tirah 1897–98* for service in the great frontier uprisings

Above: The reverse of the *India General Service Medal*, 1854–95. The attractive classically inspired design shows a winged Victory or *Nike* crowning a warrior. The clasp *North West Frontier* was awarded over a period of twenty years for several campaigns, large and small, on the Indian Frontier.

The obverse and reverse of the *India General Service Medal, 1895–1902*, here shown with single clasp *Punjab Frontier 1897–98*. The post-1902 version (for *Waziristan 1901–2*) carried the effigy and titles of Edward VII.

in those years. The campaigns were on such a large scale (36,000 troops involved in 1897–98) that many British soldiers received this medal, usually with *Relief of Chitral* for the campaign of 1895 and/or *Punjab Frontier 1897–98* and *Tirah 1897–98*, but once again it was more localised Indian units that received most of the medals and clasps (e.g. *Samana 1897* or *Malakand 1897*); the last awarded, *Waziristan 1901–2* was almost exclusively awarded to Indian troops and their British officers for service in small columns or on blockade duties. Medals with only this clasp bear on the obverse the effigy and titles of the new monarch, Edward VII. His accession in 1901 might logically have led to the introduction of a new IGS, but the old 1895 version continued to be awarded. However, in 1908 it was finally decided to issue a new type – the *India General Service Medal 1908* – which remained in use until 1935, and again rewarded service in a range of frontier campaigns. Some, like *North West Frontier 1908*, *Afghanistan and North West Frontier 1919* or *Burma 1932* were large scale and extensive affairs involving British and Indian units; others, like *Abor 1911–12*, *Mohmand 1933* or *North West Frontier*

1935 were smaller campaigns, typical of the frontier wars that had flickered for nearly a century and employing largely Indian regiments. The rarest clasp on this medal was *Waziristan 1925,* awarded only to RAF personnel who, most unusually, were given the choice of this clasp or the much more common *Waziristan 1921–24* for their service in air raids on tribes in Waziristan. The policy of using air forces to reach recalcitrant tribes in remote and distant regions (rather than sending in military columns over difficult and dangerous terrain) was just beginning to find favour and was also used in Iraq at this time.

General service medals became the norm for service all over the Empire and beyond. The *East and West Africa Medal* (1887–1900) rewarded service in expansionist and punitive expeditions on the coastal hinterlands of West Africa (especially in the Niger delta area, as with *Benin River 1894*, *Brass River 1895* and *Benin 1897*) or on the coasts of East Africa (as with *Witu 1890* and *Witu Aug. 1893*). There were twenty clasps issued, some, like *Lake Nyassa 1893*, *Juba River 1893*, *Dawkita 1897* and *Niger 1897*, being rare, since very few were awarded. Most unusually the name of one campaign on the East African coast, at *M'wele 1895–96*, was not borne on an actual clasp but engraved along the top rim of the medal. The reason for commemorating one particular expedition in this manner is unknown. Most of the recipients of these awards were locally raised African units under British officers (e.g. the Gold Coast Constabulary), volunteers from Indian regiments (especially Sikhs) and Royal Navy and Royal Marine forces landed as Naval Brigades from British warships. Apart from officers and some NCOs,

Top right: The *India General Service Medal, 1908–35.* Reverse, showing the fortress at Jamrud guarding the mouth of the famous Khyber Pass. The four clasps seen here record campaign service in Afghanistan in 1919, Waziristan (North West Frontier) and Burma.

Left: The *East and West Africa Medal, 1887–1900:* a 'general service' award for 'small wars' on the coastal hinterland of east and west Africa. Its reverse re-uses the design of the *Ashantee Medal* of 1873–74 (see p. 37). Never issued without a clasp (unlike the *Ashantee Medal*) of which two dated types are shown.

very few British soldiers were present in any number in these small tropical campaigns.

The *East and West Africa Medal* was superseded in 1902 by the long-lived *Africa General Service Medal* (1902–56), largely awarded for small campaigns in Northern Nigeria (the last phases of the British conquest of the region 1902–5) or for service in Somaliland or around the Great Lakes of East Africa. No fewer than forty-five separate clasps were issued, representing the final establishment or consolidation of British control on the coasts of west and east Africa and inland. Again, some are rare since they were issued in small numbers – like *Lango 1901* and *Kissi 1905*. Larger campaigns were those waged in Somaliland between 1901–20 against the so-called 'Mad Mullah' and involved British, Indian and African forces, as well as British warships and (in the final campaign in 1920) aircraft. No AGS medals were issued during the reign of George VI but the award was revived in 1956 with clasp *Kenya* to cover operations against the 'Mau Mau' rebellion (1956–58). Unlike most of the earlier clasps, which were awarded in small numbers mainly to locally raised African forces and are consequently rare, *Kenya* was issued in large numbers to British and local African units, the RAF, police and civilians.

The Principal General Service Medals and Clasps

Medal for Campaigns in South Africa, 1834–53

A retrospective medal authorised in November 1854 for British Army and Navy personnel involved in campaigns (originally known as the Kaffir Wars) on the South African frontiers. Three campaigns were commemorated, 1834–35, 1846–47 and 1850–53, but not indicated on the medal itself, which simply has '1853' – the date of institution. No clasps were authorised.

Medal roll:

- WO.100-17 (incomplete)
- ADM.171-18
- *The South Africa Medal Roll 1853*, G Everson (Leatherhead, Sampson, 1978).

Above: The reverse of the *Africa General Service Medal*, 1902–56. This example shows two of its many clasps, for the Somaliland campaign of 1902–4 and for the main battle in the campaign at Jidballi on 10 January 1904.

The India General Service Medal, 1854–95

Awarded for frontier campaigns and 'small wars' in the area of the Indian Empire, 1849–95. Never awarded without a clasp. Issued in bronze to Indian 'followers' and non-combatants. (See photograph on p. 65.)

Pegu	*Burma 1887–89*
Persia	(with rare variant *Burma 1887–9*)
North West Frontier	*Chin-Lushai 1889–90*
Umbeyla	*Lushai 1889–92*
Bhootan	*Samana 1891*
Looshai	*Hazara 1891*
Perak	*N E Frontier 1891*
Jowaki 1877–78	*Hunza 1891*
Naga 1879–80	*Burma 1889–92*
Burma 1885–87	*Chin Hills 1892–93*
Sikkim 1888	*Kachin Hills 1892–93*
Hazara 1888	*Waziristan 1894–95*

Medal rolls:

- WO.100-19 to 20, 42 (Artillery), 45, 69 to 75 (British regiments)

- L.Mil.5-52 to 65 (various clasps)

- ADM.171-17 (Pegu), 39 (Perak), 44 (Burma)

- *Red with Two Blue Stripes*, Col. B A H Parritt (Lusted, Tunbridge Wells, 1974): details on some of the earlier clasps.

The Canada General Service Medal, 1866–70

Awarded in silver for service against Fenian (Irish Republican) attacks along the Canadian Frontier in 1866 and again in 1870 and for the first Louis Riel rebellion ('*Red River*') in 1870. Never awarded without clasp and mainly given to local Canadian forces. Note that the medal was not actually issued until December 1899.

Fenian Raid 1866
Fenian Raid 1870
Red River 1870

Right: The *Canada General Service Medal*, 1866–70, with two of its three possible clasps. Only issued in 1899, it largely rewarded local Canadian forces for action against republican Irish (Fenian) attacks along the Canadian Frontier.

Medal rolls:

- WO.100-110
- ADM.171-35
- *The Canada General Service Medal Roll 1866–70*, R Thyen (n.p., Bunker to Bunker Books, 1998)
- *The Medal Roll of the Red River Campaign in 1870*, G N Neale and R W Irwin (Toronto, 1982).

The South Africa Medal, 1877–79

A silver medal – basically an amended version of the 1853 *South Africa Medal* (q.v.) – awarded with dated clasps for various frontier wars in South Africa, the most famous being the Zulu War of 1879. Dates reflect those of recipient's actual years of service. Medals with no clasp were awarded for 1879, largely to RN forces serving offshore or those who did not cross the Zululand Frontier. (See photograph on p. 64.)

1877	*1878*
1877–78	*1878–9*
1877–79	*1879*
1877–8–9	

An example of a Victorian medal group, showing, left to right: the *New Zealand Medal for the Maori Wars*, 1860–66, the 2nd *Afghan War Medal* without clasp, the *Egypt Medal* with clasp *Suakin 1885* for service on the Red Sea coast and the associated *Khedive's Star*, dated '1884–86'. Note the different types of 'old' or 'veiled' heads of Queen Victoria.

Medal rolls:

- WO.100-46 and 47; Royal Artillery in WO.100-54
- ADM.171-40
- *The Medal Roll for the South African War Medal 1877–8–9*, D R Forsyth (Johannesburg, 1979)
- *The Silver Wreath: the 24th Regt. at Isandhlwana and Rorke's Drift*, N Holme, (London, 1979), extended as:
- *The Noble 24th: Biographical records of the 24th Regt. in the Zulu War and South African Campaigns 1877–79*, N Holme (London, Savannah, 1999)
- *Casualty Roll for the Zulu and Basuto Wars, 1877–79*, I Tavender (London, Hayward, 1985).

The Cape of Good Hope General Service Medal, 1880–97

The silver medal awarded to local forces by the government of the Cape Colony for a series of tribal campaigns on the Cape Frontier, 1880–97. Not issued without clasp or clasps. No British troops involved.

Transkei
Basutoland
Bechaunaland

- *The Cape of Good Hope General Service Medal: The Medal Roll*, D R Forsyth (privately published, n.d.).

The East and West Africa Medal, 1887–1900

Introduced in 1892 to reward service in small-scale punitive expeditions or campaigns of conquest along the coasts of West and East Africa from 1887–1900. Not awarded without clasp. (See photograph on p. 67.)

1887–88	*Brass River 1895*
Witu 1890	*M'wele 1895 or 1895–96* (engraved on upper rim)
1891–92	*1896–98*
1892	*Niger 1897*
Witu August 1893	*Benin 1897*
Liwondi 1893	*Dawkita 1897*
Juba River 1893	*1897–98*
Lake Nyassa 1893	*1898*
1893–94	*Sierra Leone 1898–99*
Gambia 1894	*1899*
Benin River 1894	*1900*
Brass River 1895	

Medal rolls:

- ADM.171-45 (to 1892) and 46 (from 1892–98)
- ADM.171-47 (additional for M'wele 1895–96)
- ADM.171-48 (Sierra Leone 1898–99)
- *African General Service Medals*, R B Magor (Calcutta, 1978; reprinted and extended, London, Naval and Military Press, 1993).

The India General Service Medal, 1895–1902

For service on the North West Frontier of India, in various campaigns 1895–1902. Not awarded without clasp. It was issued in bronze to Indian 'followers' and non-combatants.

Defence of Chitral 1895
Relief of Chitral 1895
Punjab Frontier 1897–98
Malakand 1897
Samana 1897
Tirah 1897–98
Waziristan 1901–2

Medal rolls:

- WO.100-42 (Artillery, Chitral 1895), 78 (others, Chitral)
- WO.100-84 to 89 (other clasps, British regiments)
- WO.100-75 (Waziristan 1901–2: Europeans)
- *The Indian General Service Medal, 1895*, A Farrington (London, London Stamp Exchange, 1987): casualty roll and some dispatches.

The *India General Service Medal*, 1895–1902, in bronze. Bronze medals and clasps were awarded to Indian and some Africa non-combatants (e.g. grooms, cooks, drivers) for campaign service. After the First World War, all received the standard silver medal.

The Africa General Service Medal, 1899–1956

In 1902 it was decided to standardise awards for small-scale military expeditions in Africa with the issue of a General Service Medal. Never issued without a clasp and not awarded during the reign of George VI. Few bronze versions. (See photograph on p. 68.)

N Nigeria	*East Africa 1915*
N Nigeria 1902	*East Africa 1918*
N Nigeria 1903	*West Africa 1906*
N Nigeria 1903–4	*West Africa 1908*
N Nigeria 1904	*West Africa 1909–10*
N Nigeria 1906	*Somaliland 1901*
S Nigeria	*Somaliland 1901*
S Nigeria 1902	*Somaliland 1902–4*
S Nigeria 1902–3	*Somaliland 1908–10*
S Nigeria 1903	*Somaliland 1920*
S Nigeria 1903–4	*Jidballi* (always with *Somaliland 1902–4*)
S Nigeria 1904	*Uganda 1900*
S Nigeria 1904–5	*B.C.A. 1899–1900*
S Nigeria 1905	*Jubaland*
S Nigeria 1905–6	*Jubaland 1917–18*
Nigeria 1918	*Gambia*
East Africa 1902	*Aro 1901–2*
East Africa 1904	*Lango 1901*
East Africa 1905	*Kissi 1905*
East Africa 1906	*Nandi 1905–6*
East Africa 1913	*Shimber Berris 1914–15*
East Africa 1913–14	*Nyasaland 1915*
East Africa 1914	*Kenya*

Medal rolls:
- WO.100-91, 100 to 105, 391 to 396, 408 to 410
- ADM.171-56 and 64
- *The Africa General Service Medal to the Royal Navy and Royal Marines*, W H Fevyer and J W Wilson (London, London Stamp Exchange, 1990)
- *Africa General Service Medals*, R B Magor (Calcutta, n.d.; reprinted and extended, London, Naval and Military Press, 1993).

The India General Service Medal, 1908–35

The India General Service Medal of 1908 remained in use until 1935 and was ultimately issued with twelve clasps, all for service in India or in Burma, the majority for the North West Frontier. Never awarded without clasp, only its first two issues were granted in bronze. From then on (1912) no further bronze awards were made for Indian service. (See photograph on p. 67.)

North West Frontier 1908
Abor 1911–12
Afghanistan & NWF 1919
Mahsud 1919–20
Waziristan 1919–21
Waziristan 1921–24
Waziristan 1925
Malabar 1921–22
N W Frontier 1930–31
Burma 1930–32
Mohmand 1933
N W Frontier 1935

Medal rolls:

- WO.100-397 for *North West Frontier 1908* and *Abor 1911–12*
- WO.100-467 to 483 for *Afghanistan/NWF 1919*, *Mahsud 1919–20* and *Waziristan 1919–21* to Other Ranks
- WO.100-484 and 485 for *Afghanistan/NWF 1919*, *Mahsud 1919–20* and *Waziristan 1919–21* to officers
- WO.100-487 – clasp *Malabar*
- WO.100-488 to 492 for *Waziristan 1921–24* to British units
- WO.100-495 to 497 for *N W Frontier 1930–31*, *Burma 1930–32* and *N W Frontier 1935*
- L.Mil.7-4052: *Waziristan 1919–21* and *Mahsud* to RAF
- L.Mil.7-4056 for *Waziristan 1921–24* to RAF
- Other RAF rolls will be located in series AIR 81
- *North West Frontier 1908*, P Duckers (London, Spink, 2006): campaign history, casualty rolls, dispatches etc.
- *The India General Service Medal, 1908–35*, T Stiles (Knighton, Imperial Press, 1987): notes on all clasps.

Chapter Seven

RESEARCHING MEDALS AND THEIR RECIPIENTS, 1815–1914: A BASIC GUIDE

For references to the Internet, see Appendix 1, p. 181. The key resource for anyone wishing to trace the award of a medal or the career of its recipient is The National Archives (TNA) in Kew. Detailed guides to their resources may be read or downloaded from TNA website. The following should be consulted:

British Army Lists

British Army: Auxiliary Forces (Volunteers, Yeomanry, Territorials & Home Guard), 1769–1945)

British Army: Campaign Records, 1660–1714

British Army: Campaign Records, 1714–1815

British Army: Campaign Records, 1816–1913

British Army: Courts Martial, 17th–20th Centuries

British Army: Muster Rolls and Pay Lists, c1730–1898

British Army: Officers' Commissions

British Army: Officers' Records, 1660–1913

British Army: Soldiers' Discharge Papers, 1760–1913

British Army: Soldiers' Pensions, 1702–1913

British Army: Useful Sources for Tracing Soldiers

Medals: British Armed Services, Campaign, and other Service Medals

Merchant Seamen: Officers' Service Records, 1845–1965

Merchant Seamen: Registers of Service, 1835–1857

Ordnance, Board of (Artillery matters)

Prisoners of War, British, c1760–1919

Royal Marines: Officers' Service Records

Royal Marines: Other Ranks' Service Records
Royal Marines: How to Find a Division
Royal Marines: Further Areas of Research
Royal Naval Reserve
Royal Naval Volunteer Reserve
Royal Navy: Commissioned Officers' Pay and Pension Records
Royal Navy: Log Books and Reports of Proceedings
Royal Navy: Officers' Service Records
Royal Navy: Operational Records, 1660–1914
Royal Navy: Ratings Service Records, 1667–1923
Royal Navy: Ratings' Pension Records
Royal Navy: Warrant Officers' Pension Records

Major military museums (such as the Royal Naval Museum in Portsmouth, the National Army Museum in Chelsea, the Imperial War Museum in Lambeth, the RAF Museum in Hendon, the National Maritime Museum in Greenwich, the Royal Marines Museum in Eastney and Firepower, the Royal Artillery Museum in Woolwich) may also hold records that would be of use to researchers (e.g. ships' logbooks, squadron records, photograph albums, diaries etc.) but the range of official personal papers is very much the remit of TNA in Kew. Collections of original rolls and paperwork may also be found in the British Library, in particular those of the India Office, holding surviving papers of British – not Indian – officers and some soldiers serving in East India Company forces up to 1860 or later in the Indian army. Generally speaking, the 150 or so local or county regimental and military museums are often able to give help on the services of a particular unit but few hold any official rolls or personal records.

The researcher's first port of call should be the Documents Online section of TNA (at: www.documentsonline.nationalarchives.gov.uk), whose range of guides listed above provides a clear outline of what survives in the national record. The key here is *what survives* – researchers are often surprised to find that little remains of some archives, so that coverage of some eras or units or individuals is patchy. It should be borne in mind that institutions like the War Office or the Admiralty never saw themselves as repositories of historical or genealogical material – they produced working documents for use in their own time and when they were no longer needed (e.g. long after the death or discharge of a soldier) they were routinely 'weeded' and many were destroyed. We may regret the loss of much of these

An example of a page of WO.97 – soldiers' attestation and discharge documents. This one relates to a discharge in 1881 from the 85th Regiment. They are fairly bland in their offering of personal or biographical information.

archives, but we should, in fact, be grateful for what has actually survived this process.

Key areas of TNA records of use to the researcher of medals or military and naval service in the War Office (WO) or Admiralty (ADM) files are:

WO.97

The surviving enlistment and service records of regimental soldiers from *c.* 1754–1913. Understandably, few survive from the earliest periods and the information they provide is limited, though it can vary considerably. The detail is better (and survival rate greater) from *c.* 1880 following the Army reforms of the 1870s. Some files include medical records and punishment sheets as well as the usual listings of promotions, overseas service, campaign medals, qualifications and courses etc. Researchers new to this subject sometimes find it surprising that these records do not usually give a date of birth or a home address, though some (especially later in the nineteenth century) give details of wives and children, intended place of residence and address of next of kin.

Up to about 1883 these papers were filed only by regiment – which made it difficult to find a soldier's papers if you did not know his unit – but a cumulative index now exists. From 1883, these records are filed by surname.

WO.12 and 16

The muster and pay lists of the various regiments. If papers do not survive for 'your' man in WO.97, it is possible to provide a skeletal outline of his service in a British regiment from muster to muster and to track his movements around the country or the Empire. It helps to know roughly when the man began or ended his service and in which unit he served.

An example of a medal roll from WO.100 – in this case, for the *Queen's South Africa Medal*, listing the award of the medal and various clasps to named individuals in the 2nd King's Shropshire Light Infantry.

These lists survive in a relatively complete form – so it is much more likely that an individual can be found – but they do not tend to exist much beyond the 1880s. Similar lists survive for the Royal Artillery and other Corps.

WO.100

Army medal rolls from 1793. Rolls cover campaigns from 1793–1902 and (recently added) some of the 1918 GSM, 1902 AGS and 1936 IGS rolls, listing recipients of the various Army campaign medals and clasps by regiment. The recipient's unit has to be known in advance, unless the researcher wishes to trawl through every roll for a particular campaign!

The equivalent for medals awarded for Indian campaigns (though not usually including Indian soldiers) is L.Mil.5, held in the India Office Collections in the British Library. Those for British units often duplicate rolls also held in WO.100.

For a detailed account of the medal rolls etc. available at Kew, see *Medals: the Researcher's guide*, William Spencer (London, TNA, 2006).

ADM.29 and 73

Certificates of service for RN personnel. These cover Other Ranks service between *c*. 1802 and 1894 but they are far from complete.

ADM.36 to 39

Ships' muster and pay books from *c*. 1667–1924. Also ADM.41, 115 and 119.

ADM.53

Ships' logbooks from *c*. 1668–1925. Some contain an 'alphabet' – a nominal roll of the crew, with personal details. Some, however, do not.

ADM.139

Naval service records from 1853–73. In 1853, the principle of Continuous Service was introduced, so that men could remain in the Navy, moving straight from one ship to another, without necessarily breaking their service. Men opting for Continuous Service would initially enlist for ten years, which could be increased to twenty. The series has a nominal index.

ADM.159

Registers of services of Royal Marines. These are largely complete and detailed but can be complicated to use. Royal Marines served in Divisions – ultimately Portsmouth, Plymouth, Woolwich and Chatham – and their papers before *c*. 1880 can be difficult to locate without knowing the man's Division and his service number. The latter are sometimes given in medal rolls. Papers from 1842–1930 are now online at TNA website, but they really only cover from *c*. 1880 in detail.

ADM.171

Medal rolls for both officers and Other Ranks of naval forces. The main series of medal rolls for both officers and Other Ranks of the Navy, Merchant Navy and Royal Marines covering awards from 1793 to 1902; recently, more modern rolls (post-1918) have been added to the public collections and this process will continue over time.

A page from ADM.188, showing the service record of a sailor. They are very different from the Army records in WO.97 but are useful in listing all the ships a sailor served on, with ranks, conduct and dates.

ADM.175

Records of service of Coast Guard personnel, 1816–1947.

ADM.188

Registers of service of Other Ranks of the Royal Navy from *c*. 1873–1923. This is the most complete series of Continuous Service records, emanating from a reform of the system in 1873. The records are in a good state of completion – most were kept in large parchment ledgers not susceptible (like Army papers) to random weeding and destruction. They are available online from TNA website.

ADM.196

Service papers for RN commissioned officers, including boatswains, gunners and carpenters. Detailed records covering *c*. 1756–1926. Now available online from TNA website.

The following official Lists have been variously published in monthly, quarterly, six-monthly and annual editions. The information each contains does vary enormously in range and value to the researcher. Larger city museums as well as major military archives (like the National Army Museum) will have runs of these volumes.

The *Army List*

Published annually since 1754 and up to the present, it gives the dates of officers' promotions and appointments and enable an officer's career and movements within the service to be followed from start to finish. They are not biographical in their detail and earlier ones (pre-1870) tend to be less informative than some later ones. Later *Army Lists* (from 1881) have War Service sections and are useful for establishing or confirming an officer's campaign service, medal entitlement and awards. Quarterly Lists were published from 1879–1922 and Half-yearly Lists from 1923–50. From 1951, they have been published in three parts – current serving officers, retired officers and gradation lists with promotions, appointments etc.

Hart's Army List

Unofficial Army lists published by Colonel Hart from 1839, they are usually more detailed and informative than the official War Office versions, especially on war services. They ceased to be published in 1915. Interesting (but fragmentary) correspondence to Colonel Hart from officers regarding

| Meerut. Bengal.
Depôt, Canterbury. | **15th (*The King's*) Hussars.** | 157 |

The Crest of England within the Garter. *Merebimur.* "EMSDORF" "EGMONT-OP-ZEE" "VILLIERS EN COUCHE" "SAHAGUN" "VITTORIA" "PENINSULA" "WATERLOO."

Years' Ser.	Full Pay	Half Pay	
			Colonel.—George William Key, *Cornet*, P5 July 31; *Lt.* 25 Aug. 33; *Capt.* P16 Sept. 37; *Major*, P14 June 42; *Lt.Colonel*, 9 Feb. 47; *Colonel*, 28 Nov. 54; *Major General*, 6 Feb. 62; *Lieut.General*, 30 July 71; *General*, 1 Oct. 77; *Colonel* 15th Hussars, 19 Nov. 71.
22		...	**Lieutenant Colonel.**—George Luck,[1] *CB. Cornet*, P16 April 58; *Lt.* P20 Dec. 59; *Capt.* P9 Nov. 67; *Major*, 2 Mar. 78; *Lt.Colonel*, 29 Apr. 79.
19		...	**Major.**—Henry Langtry,[2] *Cornet*, P16 Aug. 61; *Lt.* P24 Jan. 65; *Capt.* P3 April 69; *Major*, 29 April 79.

			CAPTAINS.	CORNET.	LIEUT.	CAPTAIN.	BREV.MAJ.	BT.LT.COL.
13		...	William White[3]	P11 Jan. 67	P 1 April 68	13 May 74		
13		...	Frederick Henry Beck	P27 Feb. 67	P13 June 68	17 Jan. 75		
12		...	Henry Hall[4]	8 Jan. 68	16 Mar. 70	7 Jan. 74		
14		...	John Bullen Symes-Bullen	P22 May 66	P14 July 69	23 June 75		
12		...	George Digby Filmer Sulivan[3]	P13 June 68	28 Oct. 71	24 June 76		
11		...	Alfred Smirke[5]	P12 June 69	28 Oct. 71	2 Mar. 78		
11		...	Arthur Gambier Holland[4]	P24 July 69	28 Oct. 71	29 April 79		

			LIEUTENANTS.		LIEUT.
11		...	Arthur Thomson Middleton[3]	P31 July 69	28 Oct. 71
11		...	Cecil Francis Johnstone Douglas, *Adj.* 1 June 79	P10 Nov. 69	28 Oct. 71
8		...	John Henry Sewell,[3] *Inst. of Musk.* 7 Aug.79		8 May 72
6		...	George Allen Webbe		28 Feb. 74
6		...	Walter Joseph Burke		2 Dec. 74
6		...	Moubray Allfrey[3]		2 Dec. 74
6		...	Henry Lawrence Daly,[3] *Interpreter*		28 Feb. 74
5		...	George Fitz Austin Gavin		10 Sept. 75
4		...	*Hon.* Rupert Leigh[4]		11 Feb. 76
3		...	*Hon.* Arthur Manners[5]		6 Oct. 77
9		...	Alexander William Dennistown Campbell[3]		30 Dec. 71

			SECOND LIEUTENANTS.	2ND LIEUT.
1		...	Charles Edmund Browne	1 Jan. 79
1		...	James Redmond Patrick Gordon	22 Jan. 79
2		...	Harry Evelyn Stracey Pocklington	13 Nov. 78
1		...	Tyrell Other William Champion de Crespigny	2 July 79

21			*Paymaster.*—Roger Sheehy,[3] 13 May 59; *Honorary Major*, 13 May 74.
8		...	*Riding Master.*—David Noble Smith, 8 June 72.
11		...	*Quarter Master.*—Stephen Henry Staniland, 30 June 69.
9		...	*Veterinary Surgeon.*—Charles Whitney Gillard, 20 Sept. 71.

Blue.—*Agents*, Messrs. Cox and Co.—*Irish Agents*, Sir E. Borough, *Bt.* and Co.
Embarked for India, 14 Nov. 1869.

[1] Lt.Colonel Luck was present at the operations against the Jowaki Afreedees in January 1878. Served with the Candahar Column in the Afghan war of 1878-79, including the advance to Khelat-i-Ghilzai; commanded a squadron of the 15th Hussars and a troop of the 1st Punjaub Cavalry in engagements with the Afghan cavalry at Takht-i-Pul on the 4th January 1879 (slightly wounded, mentioned in despatches).

[2] Major Langtry served with the 3rd Dragoon Guards in the Abyssinian campaign in 1868, and was present at the storming and capture of Magdala (Medal). Served with the 15th Hussars in the Candahar Column in the Afghan war of 1878-79, including the advance to Khelat-i-Ghilzai; commanded a detached squadron of his Regiment at the affair in the Ghlo Pass, 4th January 1879.

[3] Captains White and Sulivan, Lieutenants Middleton (as Adjutant), Sewell, Allfrey, Daly, and Campbell, and Paymaster Sheehy, served with the 15th Hussars in the Candahar Column in the Afghan war of 1878-79, including the advance to Khelat-i-Ghilzai.

[4] Captains Hall and Holland and Lieut. Hon. R. Leigh served with the 15th Hussars in the Candahar Column in the Afghan war of 1878-79, including the advance to Khelat-i-Ghilzai; present in the engagements with the Afghan cavalry at Takht-i-Pul (mentioned in despatches).

[5] Captain Smirke and Lieut. the Hon. A. Manners served with the 15th Hussars in the Candahar Column in the Afghan war of 1878-79, including the advance to Khelat-i-Ghilzai, and were present at the affair in the Ghlo Pass.

A page from *Hart's Army List*, 1880, showing the officers in a particular regiment, with dates of commission, present appointment and war service.

their war service entries is held in TNA under WO.211, as is a full run of the lists themselves.

The *Navy List*

Published since 1782 as *Steel's Navy List* and officially from 1814, this is similar to the *Army List* in publishing commission and appointment dates, enabling the career of a naval officer to be followed. Later ones have detailed service sections, relating to sea and campaign service (and not simply for operations in which medals were awarded), honours and awards etc. and useful information on the ships of the Royal Navy at any one time. Still published. Unofficial Navy Lists (like *Allan's Navy Lists*) can also be found and are of variable use.

The *Indian Army List*

Brief details on Indian army officers (e.g. commission dates and present appointment) were originally published in separate compilations for the different armies of the EIC administrative divisions, the Bengal, Bombay and Madras Presidencies (e.g. the East India Register from 1844, which also contained civil appointments etc.). A combined *Indian Army List* was published from 1860 and remained in print until 1947. As with the British Army version, there were monthly, quarterly and annual versions. From 1890–1919, officers' 'war services' were included in the January editions; from 1902–42, they were included in annual supplements. War service details on Indian officers were also included in some editions.

The *London Gazette*

Gallantry medals and decorations are normally instituted by Royal Warrant (i.e. emanating from the monarch) and their award is publically announced in the *London Gazette*, an official government publication established in 1665 and still published. Here, the terms and conditions of newly established awards are laid down and can be amended as necessary, alterations equally being published in the *London Gazette*. The *London Gazette* also publishes details of officers' promotions and appointments in all services and, on occasion (e.g. some 1914–18 awards) has published citations for gallantry awards. The series is searchable online at: www.gazettes-online.co.uk.

County Record Offices and Local Libraries

These may contain not only local newspapers (old and current), with accounts of the actions, gallantry or deaths of local men, but may also hold

Numb. 21411.   **401**

The London Gazette.

Published by Authority.

TUESDAY, FEBRUARY 15, 1853.

India Board, February 14, 1853.

THE following Dispatches have been this day received at the East India House.

The Governor General of India in Council to the Secret Committee of the East India Company.

Fort William, January 5, 1853.

(Extract.)

THE annexed Dispatches from Major-General Godwin and Commodore Lambert, report the operations connected with the relief of Pegu. Our entire satisfaction has been expressed to these officers at the successful accomplishment of this service.

Major-General H. Godwin, C.B., Commanding the Forces in Ava, Arracan, and Tenasserim Provinces, to C. Allen, Esq., Secretary to the Government of India.

Sir,   *Pegu, December 15, 1852.*

IN continuation of my despatch of the 11th instant from Rangoon, I have the satisfaction to state, for the information of the Governor-General in Council, that the garrison I left at this place was relieved from its investment by the Burmese, on my arrival here yesterday at one o'clock. The strength of the enemy, added to their formidable position, the very small garrison and its falling short of ammunition, though strongly posted and with a large supply of provisions, caused me very great anxiety.

At 9 o'clock, in the night of the 11th instant, 1200 men were embarked at Rangoon in two steamers and a number of boats, and were disembarked about six miles below the Ghaut, at Pegu, on the morning of the 14th instant, and the whole ready to move off their ground by sunrise.

I had resolved to march and enter the Pagoda by the eastern gate. The last time I was here I did so by the southern gate at its capture, because the enemy from Shoegyne had marched from the east and established their batteries on that face of the Pagoda. This turned all their defences and their works on and from the banks of the river and round the Pagoda, and this move brought me directly on their rear, only having to drive in numbers of well-conducted skirmishers, and a force of about 200 men on ponies, which hung on the right flank of the column during its march, against whom, however, I hardly returned a shot.

Three miles from the Pagoda I passed a gun-carriage burning, which told me what I apprehended was the case, that finding themselves between two fires, the Pagoda and my own, their defences useless, I should find they had retired, and on coming close to the rear of their defences, and pushing on the advance, we met only a large body of skirmishers, who were gallantly repulsed by some of the Bengal and Madras Fusiliers and the Seikhs.

The march through such a close country without a road was well got over. I had with me two guns from the navy boats, drawn by a party of sailors, under Commander Shadwell, whose excessive labours were most cheerfully borne.

Our loss has been 3 killed and 9 wounded, as they had no chance of injuring us seriously. The Burmese will fight if you take your people up to the muzzle of their guns, but wisely retire when they find they are morally beaten as they ever have been in this war.

They have hidden their guns, two only have been found as yet; but in the thick grass jungle a gun is easily hidden.

I have had the aid of Brigadier-General Steel, who particularly requested to accompany me.

It was a hard day's work for all, but well accomplished; and I know few moments that have been more gratifying to me than when I met that excellent and brave officer, Major Hill, of the Madras Fusiliers, in the Pagoda.

His report cannot be prepared to-day, for there is detail respecting the admirable conduct of the Peguers, whose families came under his protection, and he has wonderfully managed to save them.

I have come the second time to Pegu, with the full intention of going onwards; as ten miles from this, at a place called Sephangoon, on the road to Shoegyne, there are the Pegu families in bond at a Burmese station there, held, for the fidelity of their husbands, in the Burmese ranks, which I hope to release to-morrow; at all events to follow the force that has been troubling this country, and break it up; but I cannot state how far I can go, as the progress of all soldiers depends upon feeding them, which can never be left to accident.

I have found more carriage than I expected here, which will assist us very much.

I have ordered a land column, under the command of Lieutenant-Colonel Sturt, of the 67th Bengal N.I., to march on the right bank of the river,—where I have been informed there is a good hackery road to Pegu,—consisting of half the Madras Horse Artillery, 50 of the Ramghur Horse, and 400 of the 67th Bengal N.I., but some local family collections of photographs, letters and ephemera and may also offer Internet facilities.

Newspapers

Local and national, these should not be neglected in the search for possible information on campaigns, individual battles, officers, soldiers, ships and ship movements, gallantry awards and casualties. The National Newspaper Archive is worth consulting; its website is accessible at: www.newspaperarchive.com.

Dealers and Auctions

These exist to supply collectors (and those wishing to obtain display examples or replacement awards) and many are listed in the collectors' magazines, such as the *Armourer* (www.armourer.co.uk.) and *Medal News* (www.tokenpublishing.com). The Internet site Medalnet (www.medal.net) offers a useful gateway to the various sites. Most leading dealers issue regular lists of items for sale, and some offer research services.

Opposite: A page of the *London Gazette*, an official publication since 1665, lists all awards, promotions and appointments in the armed services. It also publishes – as here – selected dispatches detailing recent military operations.

Chapter Eight

MEDALS FOR 'THE GREAT WAR', 1914–18

The First World War of 1914–18, once known as 'the Great War', was fought on a scale never before seen and caused casualties and damage beyond any thing yet experienced. Its military, social and economic impact was immense and unlike earlier wars in which Britain had been engaged, it involved not thousands but millions of people, military and civilian, men and women, from Britain and all over the Empire.

It was quickly agreed that the large numbers of combatants that had taken part in some of the most demanding battles in history should receive distinctive campaign medals – in addition to a whole new range of gallantry awards that were born out of the conditions of the war (see below). The question arose actually while the war was still going on as to exactly what medals should be granted and at first it was proposed to follow established precedent and award medals with appropriate campaign or battle clasps. As in earlier wars, like the Boer War of 1899–1902 for which no fewer than twenty-six clasps were issued, participation in specific actions, large or small, and in different theatres of war could then be recognised. After the war, Army and Navy committees were set up to examine the issue and proposed battle and campaign clasps that reflected the significant victories of over four years of intensive fighting. The Army came up with no fewer than seventy-nine different clasps, ranging from 'area', to campaign and individual battle clasps. The Royal Navy proposed sixty-eight of its own, including clasps for operations in support of land campaigns, like *Gallipoli Landing* and *Ostend*, major fleet actions like *Heligoland 8 Aug. 1914* and *Jutland 31 May 1916*, campaigns in designated areas, like *Baltic 1914* or *Home Seas 1918*, 'special service' operations, like *Q Ships* and *Marmora Submarines* and individual ship actions such as *Emden 9 Nov 1914* and *Konigsberg July 1915*. These would have made the medals eventually awarded for 1914–18 much more historically and personally interesting, linking their recipients with some of the most famous actions in British military history. But in the end the cost and complexity of such a procedure led to its abandonment in

1923. At a time of economic exhaustion after 1918, the matter was deemed too complex and too expensive to develop and, apart from a few specimens produced for official purposes, no full-size battle clasps were produced. The most one sees, as a mere remnant of this idea, are privately purchased miniature awards bearing some of the proposed naval clasps, the details of which were published in 1920 before the whole idea was scrapped.

Since it was decided that those who served in active operations during the 1914–18 war would receive standardised medals no matter where they served or what branch of the forces they served in, the final range of general medals for 1914–18 was quite limited. Their distribution to serving or discharged service personnel and to the next of kin of casualties was very efficiently carried out after the war, but took well into the late 1920s to complete. Some late claims and replacement awards were still being made into the 1970s, but late claims are no longer accepted.

The Army, Navy and aerial forces of Great Britain and her imperial territories and other serving organisations and civilians received the same basic campaign awards for war service, viz.:

The 1914 Star

A single-sided bronze star approved by the King for the Army in April 1917 and to naval forces in January 1918 to reward those who had served in France and Flanders on the strength of a unit from 4 August up to midnight of 22/23 November 1914. A dated clasp was instituted in 1919 to distinguish those who had been 'under the close fire of the enemy' between 5 August 1914 and 22 November.

Clasp: *Aug. 5th–Nov. 22nd.*

The 1914–15 Star

Sanctioned in 1918, this uniface bronze star is similar to the *1914 Star*, except that it carries the central dates '1914–15' in place of 'Aug–November 1914'. The *1914–15 Star* was awarded to British and imperial forces for service in any theatre of war up to 31 December 1915. No clasp is associated with this award.

The British War Medal, 1914–20

This medal (usually in silver but with some awarded in bronze) was approved in 1919 and was effectively the 'war medal' of the 1914–18 war. It was conferred on all those men and women who served in any unit of British or imperial forces, including the Mercantile Marine and some civilian categories. Its issue was extended to cover operations into 1919 in the Russian Civil War and for post-war mine-clearance at sea. No clasps were issued.

The Mercantile Marine War Medal, 1914–18

A bronze medal was authorised in July 1919 by the Board of Trade to reward members of the Merchant Navy who had undertaken one or more voyages through a designated war zone or danger area.

The Victory Medal, 1914–19

Authorised in 1919, this was awarded to those who had served in a 'theatre of war' and had received other general medals for war service. It could not be awarded by itself, so is always seen as part of a trio or simply paired with the *British War Medal*.

The Territorial Force War Medal, 1914–19

A bronze medal awarded to members of the Territorial Force (i.e. part-time soldiers and nurses) who were already members of the TF on 4 August 1914 and who had completed four years' service by that date. In addition, they had to have (a) undertaken on or before 30 September 1914 to serve overseas and (b) to have actually done so between 4 August and 11 November 1918 and (c) to have been ineligible for the *1914 Star* or *1914–15 Stars*.

The first medal instituted was the *1914 Star*, once commonly referred to (incorrectly) as 'the Mons Star'. As it was actually authorised during the war, in 1917, its ribbon is sometimes seen being worn by soldiers still on active service. The flat, uniface bronze cross bore the recipient's details (e.g. number, rank, name and unit) impressed on the reverse but was *only awarded to those who had served on the Western Front*, in France and Flanders, *prior to 22 December 1914*. This effectively meant that it was an award for the original British Expeditionary Force (BEF) which crossed over to France in August 1914 in response to the German invasion of Belgium and to its reinforcements as the campaign progressed. The original BEF was sarcastically referred to by the Kaiser as 'a contemptible little army', a name that its

The *1914 Star*, with dated clasp *5th Aug.–22nd Nov.*

men gleefully adopted as 'Old Contemptibles'. Some 378,000 of these Stars were awarded to British and Imperial forces (e.g. Indian and Canadian) and to female nurses and others in a range of support services, including the new Royal Flying Corps. Very few were awarded to the Royal Navy (since it was not conferred for service at sea), and these largely to RN personnel serving on land with naval armoured trains. They were, however, awarded to Royal Marine forces serving ashore, most famously for the defence of Antwerp and Ostend in 1914, where large numbers were captured and became prisoners of war.

Those who had served at sea in 1914 or 1915, on the Western Front after 22 December 1914 or at any time in 1915 and those who served in any other theatre of war in 1914–15 – such as Mesopotamia (Iraq), Gallipoli, Salonika or East Africa – received a different award. This was the *1914–15 Star*, authorised in 1918. Since no recipient would be allowed to receive both the *1914 Star* and the *1914–15 Star*, it was decided to make the *1914–15 Star* almost identical to the *1914 Star,* the only design difference being the central dates '1914–15' in place of 'Aug–Nov. 1914'. The medals' ribbons, too, would be identical – equal stripes of red, white and blue, representing the colours of Great Britain (and, perhaps coincidentally, those of her allies France and the USA). Approximately 2,366,000 *1914–15 Stars* were awarded to British and imperial forces.

This similarity of design – and especially of ribbon – caused some adverse comment. Those who had fought in 1914 and received the earlier Star felt that the individuality of their award was lessened, since so many more men would receive the *1914–15 Star*. From a distance, especially if ribbons alone were being worn, there would be no distinction between those who had fought since August 1914 and those who might have entered the war late in 1915. As a partial response to this, it was agreed in 1919 that a special clasp should be granted to those holders of the *1914 Star* who had been 'under the close fire of the enemy' during the crucial early stages of the campaign between 5 August 1914 and 22 November, when the lines stabilised and the German advance was halted. Accordingly, a small metal clasp bearing simply the dates *5th Aug.–22nd Nov.* was authorised. Unlike earlier campaign clasps that were securely attached to the medal

Above: The *1914–15 Star.* Approximately 2,350,000 were awarded to all fighting services, including imperial forces and to a wide range of ancillary and associated units created by the needs of a world war.

suspension, it was to be stitched directly on to the medal ribbon – an insecure expedient that led to the loss of many of the clasps, but was forced by the medal's shape. When ribbons alone were being worn recipients of the clasp wore a small silver rosette in the centre of the ribbon. The clasp and rosette at least gave some recipients of the *1914 Star* an element of distinction from those wearing the *1914–15 Star*. But since the clasp had, in most cases, to be personally claimed after the war (and one's presence in action properly confirmed) there were many who simply never bothered with it or perhaps never heard of it, so did not wear the emblem they were entitled to receive. This would also have been true of many who were killed during the war and were never awarded the clasp posthumously.

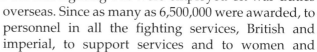

The standard medal for 1914–18 war service was the *British War Medal*, which like earlier campaign medals was made of silver. It bore on the obverse the uncrowned effigy and titles of King George V and on its reverse a symbolic design featuring a naked warrior on horseback (apparently symbolising man's control of the forces of war) trampling shields bearing the emblems of the Central Powers. The medal has the usual naming details impressed around the rim, though those to infantry officers show only the rank and name, not the unit. The medal was awarded for uniformed service anywhere in the world – though only rarely for service in Britain – and could be awarded by itself to those who had served overseas but not necessarily in a 'theatre of war'. It was, therefore, granted to those who had served on garrison duty (e.g. in India, the Far East, Gibraltar, Malta etc.) and who – through no fault of their own – saw nothing of the real fighting but were employed on war duties overseas. Since as many as 6,500,000 were awarded, to personnel in all the fighting services, British and imperial, to support services and to women and

Above: The silver reverse of the *British War Medal* for 1914–18. With approximately 6,500,000 awarded to British and imperial forces and associated units, it is the commonest British campaign medal.

Left: The bronze version of the *British War Medal*, awarded to non-combatant labour and carrying corps. It conforms to the tradition of awarding campaign medals in bronze to non-combatants, but was in fact the last such award. Approximately 110,000 awarded.

civilians, the *British War Medal* is one of the commonest British awards. Its ribbon apparently has no particular symbolic or heraldic significance.

A distinct version of this medal was produced in bronze for award to certain non-combatant units (e.g. various Labour Corps recruited from India and China and transport units like the Macedonian and Maltese Mule Corps etc.). This followed the earlier tradition of campaign awards in bronze to Indian non-combatants and was the last occasion that such awards were made. Since only approximately 110,000 were awarded, these bronze medals are now quite rare.

The third general campaign medal award for 1914–18 was the *Victory Medal*. It was awarded in addition to the Stars and *British War Medal* (and never by itself) to all those who had served in a 'theatre of war' at any time between August 1914 and November 1918 and included those who served in the Russian Civil War into 1919. This alloy medal, simply washed with a thin layer of gold paint, was universally regarded as cheap and unworthy. It is sometimes called the 'Allied Victory Medal' since the various victorious Allies all agreed that instead of conferring on each other's forces their own awards celebrating what was an Allied success, each country would produce a similar medal. Each would have an identical rainbow-striped ribbon and bear the allegorical figure of a winged Victory or warrior. In total thirteen Allied countries produced these medals and some are rare because of the small numbers of their contingents actually serving in the war. Unusually, the British medal does not bear the effigy of the monarch. Instead, the figure of Victory, with no wording, occupies the obverse, while the reverse simply has 'The Great War for Civilisation, 1914–19'. The final date was adopted to include service in the Russian Civil War, to which Britain committed large forces in 1918–19. Approximately 5,725,000 were awarded, with a special version created for South African forces in which the reverse wording was in both English and Afrikaans.

These three medals – the *1914 Star* or *1914*–15 Star, the *British War Medal* and the *Victory Medal* – really constitute the standard campaign awards for 1914–18. It should be noted that anyone who received either the *1914 Star* or the *1914–15 Star* was automatically entitled to both the *British War Medal* and the *Victory Medal* – i.e. they received three medals for their war service. It

Above: The reverse of the *Victory Medal*, its dates extended to 1919 to cover service in the Russian Civil War.

The '1914 Trio' – the *1914 Star* with dated clasp, the *British War Medal* and the *Victory Medal* – as awarded to one of the original British Expeditionary Force for overseas service from the earliest days of the war.

was, of course, possible to receive just two medals – the *British War Medal* and the *Victory Medal* – if campaign service had begun after 1 January 1916 or (as related above) simply the *British War Medal* for overseas service outside a designated campaign zone. The three medals, produced as general awards for service in some of the most horrific fighting the world has ever seen, were generally greeted with derision or at least disappointment by many of their recipients. They were regarded as cheap and tawdry – only one of them actually being in silver – and were sarcastically nicknamed 'Pip, Squeak and Wilfred' after three well-known newspaper cartoon characters of the time.

Reflecting the true nature of the conflict as a world war, these medals rewarded service not only in the familiar 'theatres' like France, Belgium, East Africa, Gallipoli, Mesopotamia, Egypt, Palestine and the Balkans (Salonika) but also in lesser known areas (some which are more or less forgotten now), including north-east Italy, West Africa, central and southern Persia, Transcaspia, the Chinese coast, the North West Frontier of India and in a multiplicity of naval operations around the world, above and below the seas. Men wearing the same set of medals could have had very different experiences of war – from 'trench warfare' and the terrible land battles of the Western Front (such as those in the Ypres Salient or on the Somme), to the deserts of the Middle East or the forests of East Africa, where climate, disease and terrain posed as great a problem as the enemy's forces, or to remote areas on the frontiers of Persia and India where it was 'business as usual' with intransigent local tribes. They may have served in the old, established arms, like cavalry, artillery and infantry, or in some of the new specialised means of warfare that came to the fore during the conflict – in submarines, tanks, airships and aircraft.

Apart from these general service awards, two others were instituted for war service. One was the *Mercantile Marine Medal*, inaugurated under the auspices of the Board of Trade. It is sometimes forgotten today that during the First World War, just as much as in the Second, maritime trade and supply between Britain and the USA and from all parts of the Empire was Britain's lifeline and that this vital link came very near to breaking in the face of highly effective German submarine (U-boat) attacks. Huge supplies of munitions, men and food poured into Britain thanks to the efforts and sacrifice of the merchant fleets and it was widely felt that those who had manned these boats should receive a distinct award. The bronze *Mercantile Marine Medal* was issued to approximately 133,200 men and some women for services in the merchant or fishing fleets in designated war zones. It is named around the rim simply with the recipient's full name, with no identification of rank or ship. Recipients also received the *British War Medal*, named in the same way, though not the *Victory Medal*. They could, of course, receive other medals for 1914–18 service if they qualified separately for them through service at some stage in another force (e.g. the Royal Navy).

The medal bears the usual titles and uncrowned effigy of George V on the obverse and a rather striking scene by Harold Stabler on the reverse – a merchant ship ploughing through heavy seas, with a sinking submarine just visible to the fore and a sailing ship in the background. Its distinctive ribbon, red and green divided by a thin white stripe, was meant to show the port and starboard lights of a merchant vessel.

Right: The reverse of the *Mercantile Marine Medal* (designed by Harold Stabler) for service in the Merchant Navy and fishing fleets, 1914–18.

A Territorial Army long-service group. The *British War* and *Victory Medals*, the *Territorial Force War Medal* and two *Territorial Efficiency Medals* – George V and George VI.

The second specialised service medal was the *Territorial Force War Medal* (TFWM). Since the soldiers of the Territorial Force were not essentially intended as an overseas' fighting force but had been called upon to volunteer for overseas service and mobilised from the earliest days of the war, it was felt that these originally part-time soldiers deserved a distinctive medal. The TFWM was awarded to those members of the Territorial Force on the outbreak of war on 4 August 1914 who had completed four years' service before that date and had agreed prior to 30 September 1914 to serve overseas (not necessarily in a war zone) and had then done so. Note that it was not issued to those Territorials who qualified for the *1914 Star* or the *1914–15 Star*. As fewer than 34,000 were issued, the TFWM is the rarest of the general awards for service during the First World War.

The medal was never awarded by itself but generally with the *British War Medal* and *Victory Medal*. However, since many Territorial units were sent to man imperial garrisons (e.g. in India or Hong Kong) to free Regular units for war service, some received only the TFWM and the *British War Medal*. The medal has the uncrowned effigy and titles of George V on the obverse and on the reverse a wreath and the simple wording 'Territorial War Medal' and 'For Voluntary Service Overseas, 1914–19'. The dates, like those on the *Victory Medal*, were presumably intended to reflect service in the Russian Civil War, but since the qualification date for this medal ceased on 11 November 1918, this must be regarded as a simple error.

In addition to actual campaign medals for war service, the government decided to recognise the sacrifice of the many who had been killed or had died during the war by conferring a distinctive *Memorial Plaque*, with associated illuminated scroll. The large bronze plaque, bearing a figure of Britannia in mourning with the 'British lion', bore the legend 'He (or She) Died for Freedom and Honour' and, in a cartouche, the full name of the casualty, but without rank, number or unit. One original intention was that these plaques could be displayed in churches, chapels or other institutions, but most were retained by the next of kin to whom they were officially issued. Some 900,000 men and over 600 women from British and imperial forces died in action during the war but in the end approximately 1,350,000 plaques were actually issued since they were also awarded in memory of those who had died of disease, or through accidents or drowning. Many died during the notorious influenza epidemic that swept the world in 1918–19.

The matter of a civilian or 'home service' medal was given serious consideration. After all, although the war was waged around the world, on land, in the air and on sea, it also drew in, more than any previous war, those on the 'home front'. We perhaps forget that tens of thousands of soldiers were engaged in such things as home-defence duties in Britain throughout the war and that civilians served in hugely expanded industries intended to increase war production, as well as in transport, training, food supply and munitions. They also suffered for the first time from direct enemy action against Britain in the form of naval bombardments and the famous Zeppelin and other air attacks. A war medal for those involved in vital war work in Britain would have been greatly welcomed, but in the end it was decided (again on the grounds of cost and complexity of administration) not to create such an award. In some ways the new *Order of the British Empire*, instituted in 1917 in a larger range of classes than was usual with British Orders, was intended to reward those in Britain and throughout the Empire who had rendered significant service to the war effort – but it could not, of course, encompass everyone who had contributed in some way and it was widely felt that an opportunity had been missed to reward the many people from all walks of life who had quietly 'done their bit' beyond the battlefields themselves. By contrast, during the Second World War, a *Defence Medal* (q.v.) for home service was actually produced.

Researching the Medals of 1914–18

The basic records are held at TNA in Kew. What follows can only be an outline guide to the extensive archives that are available on the medals, gallantry awards and service records for the First World War. Consult or download the guides available from TNA website (listed below) for detailed summaries:

British Army Lists

British Army: Auxiliary Forces (Volunteers, Yeomanry, Territorials & Home Guard), 1769–1945

British Army: Campaign Records, 1914–1918

British Army: Courts Martial: 1914–1918

British Army: Officers' Commissions

British Army: Officers' Records, 1914–1918

British Army: Soldiers' Papers, 1914–1918

First World War: Conscientious Objectors and Exemptions from Service, 1914–1918

First World War: Disability and Dependants, 1914–1918

First World War: The Conduct of the War, 1914–1918

First World War: Women's Military Services

Maps: Military Maps of the First World War, 1914–1918

Medals: British Armed Services, Campaign, and other Service Medals

Medals: British Armed Services, Gallantry

Medals: British Armed Services, Gallantry, Further Information

Merchant Seamen: Medals and Honours

Merchant Seamen: Officers' Service Records, 1845–1965

Merchant Seamen: Registers of Service, 1835–1857

Merchant Seamen: Sea Service Records, 1913–1972

Prisoners of War, British c1760–1919

Royal Air Force, RFC and RNAS Service Records: 1914–1918

Royal Air Force: Operational Records

Royal Marines: Officers' Service Records

Royal Marines: Other Ranks' Service Records

Royal Naval Reserve

Royal Naval Volunteer Reserve

Royal Navy: Commissioned Officers' Pay and Pension Records

Royal Navy: Log Books and Reports of Proceedings

Royal Navy: Officers' Service Records, 1914–1918 & Confidential Reports, 1893–1943

Royal Navy: Operational Records, 1914–1918
Royal Navy: Ratings Service Records, 1667–1923
Royal Navy: Ratings' Pension Records
Royal Navy: Warrant Officers' Pension Records
War Dead: First and Second World Wars

WO.329

The actual medal rolls for the Army and associated military units. Not available online but can be viewed at TNA. Medal rolls for the RNAS and RFC are also in this series. To locate individuals, volume and page references to this roll can be found in series WO.372 (see below).

WO.339

Records for approximately 140,000 Regular and War Service officers and RFC officers of 1914–18. Indexed in WO.338. These have survived rather better than those of Other Ranks.

WO.372

Medal Index Cards (MICs) showing medal entitlement for Army and some

A Medal Index Card (MIC), showing name, rank and unit (in this case 'Staff'), medals awarded, theatre of war first entered (France) with date. It also shows the award of 'emblems', i.e. the *Mentioned in Dispatches* oak-leaf emblem. They can be far less informative than this example.

RFC campaign service, 1914–19. A small number of cards survive here for Indian and African soldiers. Their information was drawn from the medal rolls (now in WO.329) for use by the Army Medal Office. They were originally meant simply to record a recipient's medal entitlement and the dispatch of medals and are available online via TNA website and on some commercial sites (e.g. www.ancestry.co.uk). They can be very bland (not being intended as biographical references) but nevertheless have useful information – regimental number(s), ranks and regiments served in (though without dates) and sometimes extra details, like theatre of war first entered, with date, discharge date, awards of 'mentioned in dispatches' emblems and 1914 clasp and other information such as death, with date.

WO.363

Soldiers' attestation, discharge and service papers for 1914–c. 1920. The actual records were heavily 'weeded' during the interwar years and many were destroyed. What remained was then damaged in the Blitz in 1940 and they are sometimes known as 'the burnt papers'. They can be highly informative but only about one in four sets now survives. Note that papers for those who continued to served after c. 1924 or joined after that date are still in 'closed' MoD archives and not publicly available.

WO.364

Undamaged service papers for 1914–18 and some 'reconstructed' pension documents. These two series above are available online on some commercial genealogical sites, such as www.Ancestry.co.uk.

WO.374

Records for Territorial officers (and some RFC and other non-Regulars) for 1914–18. The *Army List* will also provide limited information.

WO.95

Unit War Diaries for 1914–19. Some 10,000 War Diaries for British and imperial forces are held at TNA and are an essential reference for tracing the detailed movements and actions of a particular unit. Though it is unlikely that they will refer to an individual soldier, Officers may be frequently mentioned.

ADM.159

Service papers of the Other Ranks of the Royal Marines up to c. 1935. They are very like RN papers in the details they provide, though they also indicate shore service as well as service at sea. Now available online via TNA website.

ADM.171

Medal rolls for 1914–19 to the Royal Navy, Royal Naval Air Service (RNAS), Royal Naval Volunteer Reserve (RNVR), Royal Naval Reserve (RNR), Royal Marines (infantry and artillery) and other naval formations and associated civilians. They contain littlepersonal detail.

ADM.175

Contains records of service of Coast Guard personnel, 1816–1947.

ADM.188

Personal papers for the Other Ranks of the Royal Navy. Naval Other Ranks' records are more complete than are those for the Army. They provide some biographical information, such as place and date of birth, trade, religion, personal features (height etc.) and date of discharge, but are most interesting because they list all the ships served on, with ranks and dates – a useful resource. They are now online on TNA website.

ADM.196

Records for Royal Navy Officers from *c.* 1756–*c.* 1926. These often include detailed confidential reports and other comments. They have now been put online on TNA website.

ADM.337

Papers for Royal Naval Volunteer Reserve officers.

ADM.339

Papers for Royal Naval Reserve officers and also records of men of the Royal Naval Division, 1914–18.

AIR.1

This large archive has a variety of useful records including some for the Women's Royal Air Force, Squadron Records and Operational Records, gallantry citations, combat reports etc.

AIR.76

Records of some RFC and RAF officers, especially those who had left the service prior to 1920.

AIR.79

Service records of RAF personnel, except records for the Women's Royal Air Force, few of which survive. Apart from a few that are filed in WO.363 or 364 (standard Army papers), the main sources of personal service records for RNAS and RFC personnel are in ADM.188 and AIR.79 respectively and those for the RAF (after formation in April 1918) in AIR.79 (indexed in AIR.78). The main RAF Museum at Hendon also has some personal service records for 1914–18 RAF personnel.

As in earlier periods, officers' careers can be traced in outline via the *Army List*, *Navy List* and *RAF List*. The *RAF List* has been published since April 1918 (the date the RAF was founded as such by amalgamating the RNAS and RFC); it provides details of commission dates and appointments, but unlike the *Army List* and *Navy List*, does not offer 'war service' sections so that in general it is less informative than the Army and Navy counterparts. Still published.

BT.351

Medal rolls for the Mercantile Marine (principally the bronze *Mercantile Marine War Medal* and the silver *British War Medal*) are available in an alphabetical roll in series BT.351 at TNA.

Chapter Nine

GENERAL CAMPAIGN MEDALS OF THE TWENTIETH CENTURY

The idea of rewarding service in minor imperial campaigns with general service medals continued through the twentieth century. In 1915, a *Naval General Service Medal* (NGS) was inaugurated. Its aim was to reward Royal Navy or Royal Marine personnel for service in essentially naval operations, or those in which the Navy had significantly supported land campaigns. It ultimately had eighteen clasps, the first of which was the retrospective *Persian Gulf 1909–14*, for actions against gun-runners working between the Arabian Peninsula and the Baluchistan frontiers of British India. However, the majority of its clasps were awarded for off-shore naval service in support of land operations (e.g. *Palestine 1936–39, Palestine 1945–48, Malaya, Cyprus, Brunei* etc.) or for mine and bomb-clearance work after the Second World War (like *Minesweeping 1945–51* or *Bomb and Mine Clearance 1945–53*). A few were for specifically naval actions, the best known being *Yangtse 1949* for the famous 'Amethyst Incident' during the Chinese civil war. Medals to the ship *Amethyst* are especially sought after and awards to the other ships engaged, *London, Black Swan* and *Consort*, are also popular.

Rare clasps include *Iraq 1919–20* (to approximately 130 men serving on river gunboats), *N W Persia 1919–20* and its correctly dated replacement *N W Persia 1920*. Note that naval service off Africa (e.g. in Somaliland operations 1902–10 or 1920) was rewarded by the *Africa General Service Medal* (q.v.).

The reverse bears a fine depiction by Margaret Winser of Britannia drawn by two seahorses in a chariot of seashells through a foaming sea. Since the medal had a long lifespan, it is found with the effigy and titles of the reigning monarch current at the time of award. Only medals with the first clasp,

Right: The attractive reverse of the *Naval General Service Medal*, 1915–62. Designed by Margaret Winser. Clasp *Near East* of the Suez Crisis of 1956.

Persian Gulf 1909–14, bear the ship's name as part of the naming details; the others simply have RN or RM. Before the medal went out of use in 1962, replaced by the new *General Service Medal* of that year (q.v.), seventeen clasps had been issued. However, in 2003 it was announced that a retrospective eighteenth clasp, *Canal Zone*, would be granted to those who had served in the Suez Canal area between October 1951–October 1954 (see also *General Service Medal*, 1918–62). Multiple-clasp medals are fairly rare, though sometimes seen to Royal Marine personnel.

The land and air forces' equivalent of the 1915 NGS came in 1918 with the institution of the *General Service Medal* (GSM). This was issued for service in 'small wars' within the Empire and in areas not already covered by the India and Africa General Service Medals. The obverse bears the effigy and titles of the monarch current at the time of award and the reverse has a figure of Britannia as a winged Victory conferring a wreath on the symbolic emblems of the RAF and Army.

The medal covers a wide range of interesting and diverse operations in imperial territories around the world. Sixteen clasps were issued before the medal was replaced by the *General Service Medal* of 1962 (q.v.) but in 2003 a new retrospective seventeenth award was authorised – the clasp *Canal Zone* for those who had served in the Suez Canal zone between October 1951 and October 1954. Because of the size of the British and sometimes imperial or Indian forces engaged, most clasps are common (like *Iraq* for the Iraq rebellion of 1919–20, *Palestine 1945–48* or *Malaya*), but rarities include *Southern Desert Iraq* and *Northern Kurdistan* (both mainly to RAF recipients or local levies) and the *Bomb and Mine Clearance* clasps. Other clasps, such as *S Persia* and *N W Persia*, are not especially common to

Top: The reverse of the *General Service Medal*, 1918–62, also showing the typical back of a clasp.

Left: The retrospective clasp *Canal Zone* (1951–54) on the *General Service Medal* 1918–62. This clasp (borne on the GSM and the NGS) was only authorised in October 2003 after a prolonged campaign waged by veterans of service in the Suez Canal zone. It bears the effigy of Elizabeth II current in the 1950s.

British (as opposed to Indian) units and multiple-clasp awards with more than two clasps are unusual.

The last of the general service awards for India was the *India General Service Medal 1936–39*, issued with only two clasps, *North West Frontier 1936–37* and *North West Frontier 1937–39*. These were awarded for frontier campaigns in the perennial trouble spot of Waziristan, in particular those against the Fakir of Ipi, and, at least from the medallic point of view, mark the end of Britain's involvement with hostile frontier tribes that had been a thorn in the side of the British for almost a hundred years.

By 1962, both the *1915 Naval General Service Medal* and the *General Service Medal of 1918* were felt to be due for replacement, since as with the *India General Service Medal of 1854–95* (q.v.), it eventually became apparent that too many clasps had been awarded to one medal. The result was the institution of a new *General Service Medal* in 1962, sometimes referred to as the *Campaign Service Medal* after the plain wording 'For Campaign Service' within a wreath on its reverse. The obverse bore the usual effigy and titles of the Queen.

With the institution of this medal, separate campaign awards for the Army, Navy and Air Force ceased and personnel of these forces would receive the same campaign medal and clasps. Many of the clasps – like *Borneo* (1962–66), *Malay Peninsula* (1964–66), *South Arabia* (1964–67) and *Dhofar* (1969–76) – effectively record Britain's continued 'withdrawal from Empire', while the recent awards reflect British's ongoing military

Top: The *India General Service Medal, 1936–39*, with its two possible clasps for service on the North West Frontier. The design, featuring the Bengal tiger over a mountain landscape, is rather crude in comparison with those in the previous IGS series.

Right: Obverses of the *General Service Medal* (1918–62) with clasp *Malaya* (issued for service 1948–60) and *General Service Medal* (1962–2000) with clasp *South Arabia* (for service in and around Aden 1964–67).

involvement in world affairs, as with *Lebanon* (1983–84), *Mine Clearance – Gulf of Suez* (1984), *Gulf* (1986–89) and recent clasps for action against Iraq, like *N Iraq & S Turkey* (1991) and *Air Operations Iraq* (1991–2003). There were twelve clasps issued, with multiple-clasp awards being possible to one recipient. The most common by far is *Northern Ireland*, with over 138,000 issued; this is also the longest continually issued clasp, being current from 1969 to 2007 (see photograph on p. 121). Some of the clasps are rare, in particular *South Vietnam*, of which only seventy were awarded to Australians serving in a training role in Vietnam, 1962–64. Other clasps, as usual with British awards, are rare to certain units or rare in combination with others.

The medal was phased out in 2000, to be replaced by the *Operational Service Medal* (see below), though awards with clasps for ongoing operations, like *Northern Ireland* and *Air Operations Iraq*, continued in use beyond that date.

It was announced in 1999 that after thirty-eight years in existence the 1962 *General Service Medal* was to be replaced as of 5 May 2000 by the *Operational Service Medal* (OSM). The medal bears the tall 'Jubilee head' of the queen (first used on the commemorative *Jubilee Medal* of 1977) with the usual titles. The reverse features a central roundel in which is the Union flag, surrounded by 'For Operational Service', superimposed upon an eight-pointed star with crowns at the end of four alternate points, each representing the various armed services. The medal is named around the rim in the usual way.

The OSM was first awarded in May 2000 for thirty days' service with British peace-keeping forces in Sierra Leone during Operations *Basilica* and *Silkman* following the country's years of civil war and continued to be awarded with different time requirements for subsequent British operations in the country. It bears no clasps but has a distinctive ribbon indicating the area of service.

The new OSM was intended to be a departure from the traditional general service medals in that separate clasps would not be issued. Instead, the campaign area would be indicated only by a distinctive ribbon, as with current UN service medals. However, this idea was dropped with only the

Above: The reverse of the *General Service Medal* 1962–2000, often called the *Campaign Service Medal* because of this wording.

second award of the medal, for operations in Afghanistan following the civil war there and international intervention against the Taliban movement. It was decided in October 2003 that those forces which had been engaged 'on the ground' in Afghanistan had faced greater danger than naval and air forces operating outside the country, and that they would be granted a clasp *Afghanistan* to their medal. Those operating outside the country would receive the medal without clasp. (See photograph on p. 121.)

A further medal, with clasp bearing simply *D.R.O.C.*, was awarded to the relatively few British personnel who served in the Democratic Republic of Congo in 2003 following the civil disturbances in that country.

Principal Medals and Clasps, 1914–2008

The Naval General Service Medal, 1915–62

Instituted in 1915, this silver medal was issued for service in naval operations between 1909 and 1962. The first clasp was retrospective and covered action against gun-runners in the Persian Gulf, 1909–14.

Persian Gulf 1909–14	*Bomb and Mine Clearance 1945–53*
Iraq 1919–20	*Bomb and Mine Clearance 1945–46*
N W Persia 1919–20	*Bomb and Mine Clearance Mediterranean*
N W Persia 1920	*Malaya*
Palestine 1936–39	*Cyprus*
S E Asia 1945–46	*Near East*
Minesweeping 1945–51	*Arabian Peninsula*
Palestine 1945–48	*Brunei*
Yangtze 1949	*Canal Zone*

Medal rolls are gradually being passed into TNA under series ADM.171, but not all have yet been transferred.

- *The NGS Medal 1915–62 to the RN and RM, clasps Persian Gulf 1909–14, Iraq 1919–20, NW Persia 1920, W H Fevyer and J W Wilson* (n.p., 1995).

The obverse of the *Naval General Service Medal*, 1915–62. It shows the standard effigy of Elizabeth II used on many British campaign medals until changed to the large 'Jubilee head' in 1977.

The General Service Medal, 1918–62

This medal was the Army and RAF equivalent of the *Naval General Service Medal* (see above) and was issued for service in 'small wars' within the Empire and in areas not already covered by the India and Africa General Service Medals.

S Persia	*Palestine 1945–48*
Kurdistan	*Malaya*
Iraq	*SE Asia 1945–46*
N W Persia	*Cyprus*
Southern Desert, Iraq	*Near East*
Northern Kurdistan	*Arabian Peninsula*
Palestine (for 1936–39)	*Brunei*
Bomb and Mine Clearance 1945–49	*Canal Zone*
Bomb and Mine Clearance 1945–56	

Medal rolls are gradually being passed into TNA under series WO.100, but not all have yet been transferred. The interwar clasps are, at the time of writing, the only ones available.

- *The General Service Medal: 'Palestine 1945–48'*, David Buxton (Birmingham, 1993).

The India General Service Medal, 1936–39

The last in the series of India General Service Medals, awarded to those who served in campaigns on the North West Frontier between 1936–39. Commonly found with both clasps, especially to Indian units.

North West Frontier 1936–37
North West Frontier 1937–39

Medal rolls for British units are to be passed into TNA to join series WO.100, but have not yet been transferred.

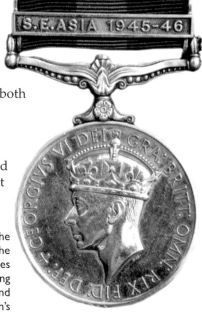

An example of one obverse type of the *General Service Medal, 1918–62*. The obverse carries a range of royal effigies and titles according to the reigning monarch at the time of the award and reflecting changes in the monarch's titles.

The Campaign Service Medal, 1962–2000

The silver *General Service Medal* of 1962, sometimes referred to as the 'Campaign Service Medal' after the wording on its reverse, replaced both the NGSM of 1915 and the GSM of 1918 and was awarded to all services.

Borneo	*Lebanon*
Radfan	*Mine Clearance*
South Arabia	*Gulf*
Malay Peninsula	*Kuwait*
South Vietnam	*N Iraq and S Turkey*
Northern Ireland	*Air Operations Iraq*
Dhofar	

Medal rolls: not available.

The Operational Service Medal, 2000–to date

After thirty-eight years in existence the 1962 *General Service Medal* was replaced as of 5 May 2000 by the *Operational Service Medal*. Distinctive ribbons and/or clasps so far awarded for:

Sierra Leone (no clasp)
Afghanistan, without clasp
Afghanistan, with clasp *Afghanistan*
Democratic Republic of Congo, with clasp *D.R.O.C.*

Medal rolls: not available.

Chapter Ten

MEDALS FOR THE SECOND WORLD WAR, 1939–45

When it came to awarding campaign medals for service in the Second World War, the authorities were faced with the same problem as in 1918: how to reward adequately and commemorate service in a long and complex conflict that had covered large areas of the globe and drawn in other imperial territories and the civilian population of Britain. Just as with the First World War, there was the possibility of producing a large range of campaign and battle awards, but, equally as with 1914–18, it would prove impossible to commemorate all the battles, actions and incidents that regiments, corps and units – let alone national opinion – might regard as vital or significant.

The result was much the same as for the First World War: medals would be issued on a 'general' basis, in this case theatre by theatre, rather than seeking to reward individually a multiplicity of actions and engagements. In the end, a series of eight campaign stars and two medals was issued, some with specific clasps, with a complex series of award criteria that can make for confusing reading. They were awarded to all British and Commonwealth forces, including the Merchant Navies, and to a wide variety of civilian, para-military, medical and other services.

Eight different campaign stars, in copper-zinc alloy, were awarded for service during the Second World War. The obverse designs are identical, except for the 'theatre' wording, and the reverse is plain.

1939–45 Star – possible clasp *Battle of Britain*.
Atlantic Star – possible clasps *Air Crew Europe* or *France and Germany*.
Air Crew Europe Star – possible clasps *Atlantic* or *France and Germany*.
Africa Star – possible clasps *North Africa 1942–43* or *8th Army* or *1st Army*.
Pacific Star – possible clasp *Burma*.
Burma Star – possible clasp *Pacific*.
Italy Star – no clasps awarded.
France and Germany Star – possible clasp *Atlantic*.

1. 1939–45 Star

This was the basic 'overseas' service' award, not conferred for home service (except for RAF Battle of Britain aircrew) or service not in 'a theatre of war'. Its conditions of award varied from service to service. It was originally to be dated '1939–43' (i.e. to the end of the North Africa campaign) but was extended to 1945 to cover other campaigns in Italy, North West Europe and the Far East. Its award was authorised during the war, so that forces' personnel are sometimes seen wearing its ribbon (all they got at first!) while the war was still going on. Its ribbon, with equal stripes of dark blue, red and light blue, represents the three fighting services (Royal Navy, Army and Air Forces).

Possible clasp: *Battle of Britain*.

2. Atlantic Star

This star was primarily intended to reward the services of the Merchant Navy and their escorting Royal Navy warships in the arduous battle of the Atlantic. Waged against powerful German U-boat fleets in the vital work of operating supply and personnel convoys and for service on the difficult Russian Convoys, it was also awarded to RAF crews on escort duties (e.g. Coastal Command) and to soldiers serving on armed merchant ships (e.g. Royal Artillery gunners). The moiré ribbon in shades of white, yellow and green represents the seas of the North Atlantic.

A Second World War group, showing typical campaign stars and the two war medals, left to right: the *1939–45 Star*, the *Africa Star*, the *Italy Star*, the *Defence Medal* and the *War Medal*.

Possible clasps: *Air Crew Europe* or *France and Germany*.

3. Air Crew Europe Star

This, the rarest of the general awards for the Second World War, was conferred largely on crews of Bomber Command and escorting fighter squadrons for raids over Nazi Germany and the occupied territories of Europe prior to the Normandy Landings in June 1944.

Possible clasps: *Atlantic* or *France and Germany*.

4. Africa Star

This star was principally awarded for service between 10 June 1940 and 12 May 1943 in North and North East Africa (Ethiopia, Italian Somaliland, Eritrea, Egypt, Libya, Tunisia etc.) and also in Malta, but not for West Africa or Madagascar. Its ribbon stripes of dark blue, dark red and light blue represented the three principal armed services, on a background of sandy yellow representing the desert.

Possible clasps: *North Africa 1942–42* or *1st Army* or *8th Army*.

5. Pacific Star

The campaign star for service in the Pacific theatre, December 1941–September 1945. It was largely awarded to British naval forces serving with US formations in the Pacific and to Australian and New Zealand forces. It was also granted for service in Hong Kong prior to its capture by the Japanese in December 1941, in Malaya before the fall of Singapore in February 1942, in the Pacific islands and in China, 1941–42. Its colourful ribbon stripes again represent the colours of the three principal service (dark blue for the Navy, red for the Army and light blue for the Air Force) with additional stripes of green (representing the forests) and yellow (the beaches).

Possible clasp: *Burma*.

6. Burma Star

Awarded to British and Commonwealth forces, military, naval, air and mercantile, for the campaign of December 1941–September 1945 to re-conquer Burma and drive out its Japanese occupiers. Despite its name, the *Burma Star* was also awarded for service in eastern Bengal and Assam, 1942–43, in China and in Malaya (after February 1942). It is interesting to note that service in Malaya in 1941–42 prior to the fall of Singapore was rewarded with the *Pacific Star*! The ribbon stripes of dark blue, red and light blue again recall the principal armed services, with an orange band representing the tropical sun.

Possible clasp: *Pacific*.

7. Italy Star

Despite its title, this star was awarded for service in a range of theatres beyond the main Italy campaign of 1943–45. It was also conferred for operations in Sardinia, Corsica, southern France, the Aegean and Dodecanese Islands, Yugoslavia, Greece and Austria. Its ribbon stripes represent the heraldic colours of the House of Savoy, the royal family that united Italy in the period 1860–71 and had ruled since then.

No clasps were awarded with this medal.

8. France and Germany Star

Awarded for the North West Europe campaign beginning with the D-Day landings in June 1944 and up until the final surrender of Germany in May 1945. Despite its title, it was also awarded for service in Belgium and Holland. Its ribbon colours, simple stripes of red, white and blue, represent the heraldic colours of Great Britain, France and Holland.

Possible clasp: *Atlantic*.

Defence Medal

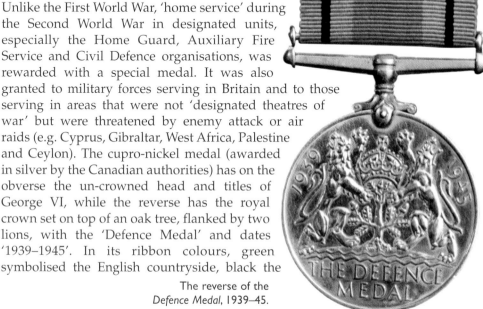

Unlike the First World War, 'home service' during the Second World War in designated units, especially the Home Guard, Auxiliary Fire Service and Civil Defence organisations, was rewarded with a special medal. It was also granted to military forces serving in Britain and to those serving in areas that were not 'designated theatres of war' but were threatened by enemy attack or air raids (e.g. Cyprus, Gibraltar, West Africa, Palestine and Ceylon). The cupro-nickel medal (awarded in silver by the Canadian authorities) has on the obverse the un-crowned head and titles of George VI, while the reverse has the royal crown set on top of an oak tree, flanked by two lions, with the 'Defence Medal' and dates '1939–1945'. In its ribbon colours, green symbolised the English countryside, black the

The reverse of the
Defence Medal, 1939–45.

wartime black-out and orange the flames of bombing raids.

Issued unnamed (like the other Second World War general awards) it has no associated clasps.

1939–45 War Medal

The standard medal (as opposed to Star) for 1939–45 service, this cupro-nickel award was granted for twenty-eight days' operational or non-operational service in the full-time armed services. Like the *Defence Medal*, it was awarded in silver by the Canadian authorities. Its ribbon, again using red, white and blue stripes, represents the colours of the Union flag – as well as those of France and the USA. The obverse bears the 'crowned head' effigy of George VI with titles, while the obverse has the dates '1939–45' and a symbolic design with a lion standing over a double-headed dragon.

Issued unnamed (like the other Second World War general awards) it has no associated clasps, but those who were *Mentioned in Dispatches* (see below) for any service or theatre of war wore a single bronze oak-leaf emblem on the ribbon of this award, not on the campaign stars or *Defence Medal*. It should be noted that only one oak-leaf emblem was worn, no matter how many times the recipient was 'mentioned'.

General

The Stars were uniface (i.e. with no design on the reverse) and made of pressed copper-zinc alloy, issued unnamed. The two medals were struck in cupro-nickel, similarly unnamed. As usual with medals issued unnamed, it is quite common to see awards that have been privately named. The whole series has always been regarded as somewhat cheap and lacklustre, but the fact is that economic considerations governed their production; the financial and industrial ruin of Britain after the Second World War and the

Top right: The symbolic reverse of the *War Medal* for 1939–45.

Left: An example of a campaign star for Second World War service, in this case the *1939–45 Star*, the basic award for campaign service overseas given in addition to more specific area stars.

immense demands on her economy in the face of post-war reconstruction did not allow for any greater expenditure.

It is evident that the 'theatre' names given to the various campaign awards were not really appropriate in many cases – and were another cause for complaint. For example, the *Italy Star* was awarded not only for service in the Italian campaign of 1943–45, but also for the invasion of Southern France, operations in the Aegean and Dodecanese Islands, Greece, Corsica, Yugoslavia and Austria. It might better have been called the 'Mediterranean Star'. Similarly, the *Pacific Star* and the *Burma Star* were both awarded for service in Malaya (the former for service prior to the fall of Singapore in 1942 and the latter for its reconquest after 1943) and the *France and Germany Star* was also awarded for service in Belgium and Holland. Personnel who had never served in Italy, the Pacific, Burma or France might wear medals bearing only those place names! It might have been better to generalise the titles even further to 'Northern European Star' or 'Far East Star', but that is another story!

The Issue of Campaign Clasps

The vexed matter of battle or campaign clasps naturally raised its head after 1945, as it had after 1918, and there was no shortage of particular actions that might have been commemorated. For example, should distinctive awards or clasps be given for important victories like the sinking of the *Bismarck*, El Alamein, the D-Day Landings, Kohima or Monte Cassino – to name but a few – or campaigns like Norway, Crete or Anzio etc.?

In the end, it was decided to award clasps to some of the Stars, but on the grounds of cost and complexity only on a limited and generalised basis. These were uniface gilt metal bars simply stitched on to the ribbon of the appropriate Star (as with the clasp to the *1914 Star*) and only one clasp, the first actually earned, could be worn on any one Star.

The rare clasp *Battle of Britain*, worn only on the *1939–45 Star*, was awarded to aircrew of squadrons actually engaged during the vital air war over Britain in 1940–41. When ribbons alone were worn, it was represented by a gilt rosette – not silver as with some other clasps. This rare and sought-after clasp has been heavily faked.

For the *Africa Star*, three clasps were approved. *North Africa 1942–43* was granted largely to Royal Navy, Merchant Navy and RAF units operating over or off North Africa during that period. Recipients of this clasp wore a single silver rosette on the ribbon when ribbons alone were being worn. The clasps *1st Army* or *8th Army* were awarded to personnel of those forces and when ribbons alone were worn, their possession was indicated by a small white-metal numeral *1* or *8* on the ribbon.

Clasps were also award for other Stars. The clasp *Atlantic* could be worn on the ribbon of the *Air Crew Europe* or *France and Germany* Stars, *Burma* could be worn on the *Pacific Star*, *Pacific* could be worn with the *Burma Star*, *France and Germany* could be worn on the *Atlantic* or *Air Crew Europe* Stars (for service after 6 June 1944) and *Air Crew Europe* worn with the *Atlantic Star* – largely earned by aircrew of Coastal Command. In all these instances, the possession of a clasp would be indicated by a small silver rosette when ribbons alone were worn. There were no clasps for the *Italy Star*.

In all cases, recipients would receive the Star they had first earned, then the appropriate clasp (if they qualified for one) but they could not wear more than one clasp on any Star. (See example on p. 157.)

It should be noted that some Commonwealth Dominions and territories awarded their own distinctive war medal (though their forces also received the general British campaign awards) – Australia, New Zealand, India, Southern Rhodesia, Canada and South Africa (in the last instance, one for home and one for overseas' service); as late as 1981, Newfoundland issued a retrospective medal for 1939–45 service, since it was not technically covered by the Canadian version.

Medal rolls: not available.

Personal and service records for all branches are not currently in the public domain, but are still held by the appropriate service archive.

Since the medals were issued unnamed, unless privately engraved or impressed, they can only be researched if they are from a documented source or are accompanied with other named campaign medals, long-service awards or decorations to the same recipient. However, personal service papers for those serving in the Second World War are still held in closed official archives and only available to the recipient or authorised next of kin.

Chapter Eleven

MEDALS FOR MAJOR CAMPAIGNS AFTER 1945

Apart from the ongoing award of the 1915 NGS and 1918 GSM for 'small wars' or limited operations, medals were of course awarded for the larger campaigns in which British forces were engaged after 1945.

The first post-war conflict of significance was 'the first United Nations War' in Korea, 1951–53; it was also the first Great Power conflict in the nuclear age and the first of the reign of Queen Elizabeth II. The cupro-nickel campaign medal was awarded for only one day's service ashore or twenty-eight days offshore to British and Commonwealth forces, though the Union of South Africa issued its own medal for the campaign. It bore on the obverse the uncrowned head of the Queen (whose Coronation had not taken place at the time the award was instituted) and titles; two versions exist – the first version with 'Br. Omn.' in the legend and the rarer second type without. The medal awarded to Canadian forces was produced in silver and also had 'CANADA' on the obverse. The reverse, designed by the prolific E Carter Preston, showed Hercules fighting the Hydra, symbolising the attempt to hold back the 'many headed monster' of Communism.

Medals to the Gloucester Regiment are most sought after because of their famous action on the Imjin River and medals to the RAF (mainly to Sunderland flying boat crews of the Far East Flying Boat Wing) are rare.

The first *United Nations Medal* was that awarded for service in the Korean War. It was given to all those who

Above: The reverse of the cupro-nickel *Medal for the Korean War*, 1951–53, by E Carter Preston – a Liverpool sculptor who designed a number of British campaign medals.

Left: The obverse of the UN medal for Korea, 1951–54. This design – the badge of the UN – has been used on all UN medals up to the present time.

served in UN forces in Korea or in support units in Japan for one day during the war. Its issue was extended up to 27 July 1954, so it is sometimes seen without the British award, entitlement to which ended in July 1953. The bronze-alloy medal is very thin and bears on its obverse the UN badge (a projection of a world map within a wreath) and on the reverse the wording 'For Service in Defence of the Principles of the Charter of the United Nations' (and versions in eleven other languages reflecting the diversity of the UN forces engaged in Korea). The clasp *Korea* was integral to the award. The medal was rather too thin to be named, but some issued to Canadian forces were named in small block capitals. Since 1954, UN medals (a standardised design differentiated generally by varied ribbon colours for different campaigns) have been issued to British forces for service in many different operations since Korea – most commonly for Cyprus and Bosnia. Over sixty different types have so far been awarded.

Apart from awards of the 1918 GSM and 1962 GSM, mainly for 'retreat from Empire' operations, such as those in Malaysia, Cyprus, Borneo, Aden etc., the next major campaign to produce a separate medal was the South Atlantic or Falklands War in 1982. The *South Atlantic Medal* was awarded for the re-conquest of the Falkland Islands following the Argentine invasion in April 1982. Largely for political reasons, it was perhaps the most rapidly produced and issued of all modern British campaign medals. The cupro-nickel medal, the watered blue, white and green ribbon of which echoes that of the *Atlantic Star* (q.v.), was granted for at least one full day's service in the Falklands or South Georgia or thirty days in the operational zone, which included Ascension Island. Those who served ashore or south of Ascension Island wear a large silver rosette on the actual medal ribbon. Its obverse was the first campaign medal to carry the new 'Jubilee head' of the Queen – first used on the commemorative *Jubilee Medal* of 1977 – while the reverse depicts the arms of the Falklands.

Awards to the Scots Guards, Welsh Guards and Parachute Regiment and to some naval vessels (e.g. the submarine *Centurion*, which sank the Argentine battleship *General Belgrano*) can command high prices. Unusually for modern British medals, those awarded to Royal Navy ships (but not

Above: The *South Atlantic Medal* for the Falklands War, 1982. Reverse, showing the coat of arms of the colony. The silver rosette indicates service south of Ascension Island or on the Falklands themselves.

Merchant Navy vessels) include the name of the ship in the impressed naming details.

The cupro-nickel *Gulf War Medal* was awarded to British forces that took part in operations on Kuwait and Iraq following the Iraqi attack on Kuwait in August 1990, or in associated support roles. For those who served in the invasion of January–February 1991, seven days' service was required; otherwise the basic requirement was thirty days' continuous service in Kuwait or in other parts of the Middle East (e.g. Cyprus) with support services. A large number of civilians received the award for serving in administrative and support roles, backing up the fighting forces.

The obverse has the now-standard 'Jubilee head' of the Queen with the usual titles. The reverse has symbols of the combined services – an anchor, an automatic rifle and the RAF eagle motif – with 'the Gulf War' above and dates '1990–91' below. Two clasps were issued. The very rare *2 Aug. 1990* was awarded to the few

Above: The reverse of the *Gulf War Medal*, 1990–91, with symbols of the three armed services. With dated clasp.

Below: A modern campaign medal group with, left to right: the *Gulf War Medal* of 1990–91, with dated clasp, the UN medal for Bosnia and two NATO service medals – for *Former Yugoslavia* and *Kosovo*. The 'Jubilee head' is shown at far left.

British service personnel who were in Kuwait (as the Kuwait Liaison Team) at the time of the Iraqi invasion. The clasp *16 Jan. to 28 Feb. 1991* was granted to those who actually crossed into Iraq as part of the invasion force. When ribbons alone are worn, the clasp is represented by a silver rosette. The ribbon is yellow (representing the desert) flanked on both sides by stripes of dark blue (representing the Navy), red (the Army) and light blue (the RAF). More than 45,000 medals were issued, with naming details in impressed capitals around the rim. Most recipients also received the associated Saudi Arabian and Kuwaiti medals for the campaign, though they were not allowed to wear them in uniform – unlike the situation that pertained in the nineteenth century when British forces were freely allowed to accept and wear in uniform allied awards like the Turkish medals for the Crimea and the Khedive of Egypt's awards for 1882–98 (q.v.).

Apart from continuing awards of the 1962 GSM and the new OSM (see above), the last campaign to date to receive a distinctive campaign medal is that for the Iraq War, which began in 2003. The *Iraq Medal* was awarded to British forces that took part in the international operation to depose Saddam Hussein and establish a democratic government in Iraq. The medal, in cupro-nickel, was designed by Major (Retd) M Atkinson of the Army Medal Office and features on its reverse a figure of the legendary Lamassu, the human-headed winged bull of Assyrian mythology above the word 'Iraq'. The design is reminiscent of the *Egypt Medal* of 1882 (q.v.). The obverse has the now standard effigy and titles of the monarch. One clasp *19th Mar. to 28th Apr. 2003* was issued to all those who took part in the actual invasion of Iraq (*Operation Telic*). Those who served in Iraq after that date received the medal without clasp. The naming on the first awards was machine impressed in the usual way, but later issues are engraved using a new laser-engraving machine – the first time British medals have been named in this way. (See photograph on p. 122.)

Medals for Post-war Service

The Medal for the Korean War, 1951–53

The cupro-nickel medal bore on the obverse the uncrowned head of the Queen and titles. The medal awarded to Canadian forces was produced in silver and also had 'CANADA' on the obverse. (See photograph on p. 115.)

Medal rolls and service records not publically available.

- *Casualties sustained by the British Army in the Korean War, 1950–53*, London Stamp Exchange (London, n.d.).

The United Nations Medal for the Korean War, 1951–53.

The first UN medal was that awarded for service in the Korean War, given to all those who served in UN forces in Korea or in support units in Japan. Its issue was extended up to 27 July 1954. Many copies of the British version have appeared on the market in recent years. (See photograph on p. 115.)

The United Nations Emergency Service Medal, 1956–67

A medal was awarded by the UN to personnel who served with the Emergency Force that patrolled the Egypt–Israel border in the Sinai desert to police a cease-fire after the war of 1956. Medals were issued to a number of participating countries as well as Britain, e.g. Brazil, Canada, Finland and others. It has the standard UN obverse – a map of the globe within a wreath – but with 'UNEF' at the top. The reverse has the standard wording 'In the Service of Peace'. The medal hangs from a ring suspension.

The Rhodesia Medal, 1980

A medal was issued to approximately 2,500 British service and associated personnel (e.g. British police) who served in Rhodesia for at least fourteen days between 1 December 1979 and 20 March 1980 to monitor the elections. They ended a long period of conflict between Ian Smith's government (which had declared independence from Britain in 1967) and nationalist groups. The result was the emergence of the independent Republic of Zimbabwe under Robert Mugabe. The medal bears the 'Jubilee head' of the Queen and usual titles on the obverse. The reverse has a sable antelope below the words 'The Rhodesia Medal' and the date '1980'. The cupro-nickel medal was rhodium plated, which gives it an unusual hardness and sheen.

The South Atlantic Medal for Falklands Campaign, 1982

The medal awarded for the re-conquest of the Falkland Islands following the Argentine invasion in April 1982. No clasps were awarded, but a large silver rosette is borne on the ribbon by those who served south of Ascension Island or on the Falkands themselves. Medal rolls and service records not available. (See photograph on p. 116.)

Medals for Service with the United Nations, 1948–to date

The first United Nations medals awarded to British forces were those for Korea and later on Cyprus. However, in recent years, British forces have been involved in many UN operations around the world (e.g. in Bosnia) and have qualified for a wide range of UN service awards. Over sixty have been issued to date. The medals, made of bronze alloy, are standardised for all operations and have the UN badge on the obverse and, in the English version, the words 'In the Service of Peace' on the reverse. The medals are distinguished by different coloured ribbons for each operational area and in some cases by the award of a clasp (e.g. CONGO or an acronym based on the formal UN title for the operation). Eligibility is, by modern award standards, quite long – commonly 90 days' service or in some cases 180 days. For subsequent tours of duty of six months in the same operational area, a silver numeral is worn on the ribbon denoting how many tours have been completed.

The Medal for the Gulf War, 1991

A cupro-nickel medal was awarded to British forces that took part in operations in Kuwait and Iraq following the Iraqi attack in Kuwait in August 1990, or in associated support roles. Awarded with one of two clasps or without clasp. When ribbons alone are worn, the clasp is represented by a silver rosette. (See photograph on p. 117.)

> *2 Aug. 1990* – awarded to the few British service personnel who were in Kuwait (as the Kuwait Liaison Team) at the time of the Iraqi invasion.
> *16 Jan. to 28 Feb. 1991* – to those who actually crossed into Iraq as part of the invasion force.

Medal rolls and service records not available.

NATO Service Medals, 1994–to date

With NATO forces being deployed further afield than ever before, a range of NATO service medals was instituted in 1994. These are awarded to British forces serving as part of NATO deployments but are not awarded along with UN medals for the same operational zone or if separate British campaign awards have been made. The thin medals are made of the alloy tombac and have standardised obverse and reverse designs. The obverse has the NATO emblem of the North Star within a wreath and the reverse has the wording 'In Service of Peace and Freedom / Au service de la Paix et de la Liberte'. Around the circumference are the words 'North Atlantic Treaty Organisaion / Organisation du Traite de l'Atlantique du Nord'.

The operational area is designated by the ribbon (usually in combinations of NATO's colours, blue and white or silver), each having its own distinctive design, and/or by clasps worn on the ribbon. The time requirement for the award is generally thirty days' service in the actual zone or ninety days in support operations outside the area. (See photograph on p. 117.)

NATO medals awarded to British troops include those for service in the aftermath of the Balkan Wars of the 1990s:

1. With distinctive ribbon and clasp *Former Yugoslavia*.
2. With distinctive ribbon and clasp *Kosovo*.
3. With clasp *Article 5* and two distinctive ribbons for operations 'Eagle Assist' (air surveillance) and 'Active Endeavour' (naval support operations).
4. With distinctive ribbon (but no clasp) for service in Macedonia.
5. With distinctive ribbon and clasp *Non Article 5* – from December 2002 replacing the earlier *Former Yugoslavia*, *Kosovo* and *Article 5* awards.

As with UN medals, those who have taken part in multiple tours in the same zone wear a small white-metal numeral on the ribbon to denote the number of tours.

A modern campaign group, showing, left to right: the NATO service medal for *Former Yugoslavia*, the 1962 *General Service Medal* with clasp *Northern Ireland* and the new *Operational Service Medal* (OSM) with ribbon and clasp for *Afghanistan*.

The Medal for the Iraq War, 2003–to date

The *Iraq Medal* was awarded to British forces that took part in the international operation to depose Saddam Hussein and establish a democratic government in Iraq.

Without clasp
With clasp *19th Mar. to 28th Apr. 2003.*
Medal rolls and service records are not available.

The reverse of *Iraq Medal* (2003–to date), with dated clasp. The ribbon has the colours of the three principal armed services of a background on sandy yellow, representing the desert.

Chapter Twelve

RESEARCHING MEDALS AND THEIR RECIPIENTS, 1920–2008

It is not possible at present to do much research into medal rolls, individual entitlement and personal service records for those serving after *c.* 1924. Many records remain in 'closed' official archives. The following detailed guides can be read or downloaded from TNA website:

British Army Lists

British Army: Auxiliary Forces (Volunteers, Yeomanry, Territorials & Home Guard), 1769–1945

British Army: Campaign Records, 1939–1945, Second World War

British Army: Campaign Records, 1945–

British Army: Courts Martial, 17th–20th Centuries

British Army: Useful Sources for Tracing Soldiers

Maps: Military Maps of the Second World War, 1939–1945

Medals: British Armed Services, Campaign, and other Service Medals

Medals: British Armed Services, Gallantry

Medals: British Armed Services, Gallantry, Further Information

Medals: Civilian Gallantry

Merchant Seamen: Medals and Honours

Merchant Seamen: Officers' Service Records, 1845–1965

Merchant Seamen: Sea Service Records, 1913–1972

Prisoners of War, British, 1939–1953

Royal Air Force Service Records: Second World War, 1939–1945

Royal Air Force: Operational Records

Royal Marines: Officers' Service Records

Royal Marines: Other Ranks' Service Records

Royal Naval Reserve

Royal Naval Volunteer Reserve

Royal Navy: Commissioned Officers' Pay and Pension Records

Royal Navy: Log Books and Reports of Proceedings

Royal Navy: Operational Records, 1660–1914

Royal Navy: Operational Records, Second World War, 1939–1945

Royal Navy: Operations and Policy after 1945

Royal Navy: Ratings' Pension Records

Royal Navy: Warrant Officers' Pension Records

Second World War: Home Front, 1939–1945

War Dead: First and Second World Wars

Medal rolls covering the campaigns of the twentieth century after *c*. 1920 are not fully accessible to researchers. Only some are available at TNA – in the WO.100 series for earlier clasps on the GSM 1915–62, currently up to *Palestine* (1936–39), and under ADM.171 for some of the earlier clasps for the NGS 1915–62. The process of transferring to TNA the rolls for other clasps and for the IGS 1936–39 is underway, and they will in due course appear in the appropriate record series.

The same is true for medal rolls (actually index cards) for 1939–45: the existing records are not open to the public. The combined Ministry of Defence Medal Office has recently been created, moving the separate Army, RAF and RN medal offices from their former sites (e.g. the Army Medal Office in Droitwich) to a new location at RAF Innsworth, Gloucester, GL3 1EZ. However, the Medal Office will not usually give information on entitlement or issue unless to the actual recipient or proven next of kin.

For honours and awards, information is generally more easily available. Locating the date of award in the *London Gazette* is the best place to start (online at: www.gazettes-online.co.uk). After that, each of the major services – Army, Navy and RAF – has its own archive series (and in some cases several) in TNA relating to the award of gallantry and distinguished service medals. (See the online guides to research at TNA, listed above.).

WO.215

War Diaries for British and Commonwealth forces, 1939–45.

WO.373

Army honours and awards for British and Commonwealth forces from 1935 to *c*. 1993. These are original recommendations, mainly listed by operational theatre, from which awards were ultimately derived. It should be noted that they are not complete – some have not survived – but they are frequently more detailed than any published 'citation' for the award. They are available online via TNA website.

ADM.171-164 and 165

Gazette dates for Royal Navy and Royal Marines honours, 1942–72. ADM.171-164 has awards from 1942–46 and ADM.171-165 has awards 1946–72.

ADM.1

Details of operations leading to awards. Actual details on the operations that led to the awards may be located in ADM.1, with some also in ADM.116 and a few in ADM.199.

AIR.2

For RAF honours, 1939–45. This series also covers Commonwealth aerial forces. The files contain recommendations for awards that were ultimately not granted as well as for those actually conferred, but at present there is no nominal index to this large series so that locating what could be interesting information is difficult. A keyword search of AIR.2 is possible online via TNA website.

AIR.50

Combat reports for 1939–45. RAF and Royal Navy operational records for most British and Commonwealth forces for the Second World War are available at TNA and are now accessible online at TNA website.

BT.395

Board of Trade medal rolls for Merchant Navy service, 1939–45.

It is hoped that personal papers relating to Home Guard service 1939–45 (currently in store) will be digitised and put online in the near future.

The MoD archives that hold personal records for those serving after *c.* 1924 are not open to public use and remain 'closed' to other than the personnel themselves or the next of kin of deceased soldiers.

Medal rolls and service records for major post-war operations (from Korea to Iraq 2003) are equally in MoD archives that are not available to public scrutiny. 'Closed' Army records for persons serving after *c.* 1924 are held in Army Historic Disclosures, Mailpoint 555 (for deceased personnel), Kentigern House, Brown Street, Glasgow, G2 8EX. Again, only bona fide next of kin may be given copies of records. The same is true of RAF personnel records held at RAF Innsworth and naval records held by The Directorate of Personnel Support (Navy), TNT Archive Services, Tetron Point, William Nadin Way, Swadlincote, Derbyshire.

Chapter Thirteen

THE ORIGINS OF BRITISH GALLANTRY AWARDS

As with campaign medals, there was no national system of reward for those whose gallantry in action was recognised by their leaders or comrades. The earliest known British awards specifically for bravery in battle are the oval gold medals awarded to Robert Welch and John Smith for their actions at the battle of Edgehill in October 1642, where they recovered the Royal standard and captured two pieces of enemy artillery. Both were knighted for their services. The Royal Warrant authorising the medal to Welch and his actual medal still survive; presumably that to Smith was much the same. The award was designed by the renowned engraver Thomas Rawlins and featured on the obverse the conjoined busts of Charles I and Prince Charles and on the reverse the Royal standard that Welch had saved. It is reported that the medals were worn around the neck from green ribbons, so that the idea of wearing a medal from a coloured band was established early on. Other contemporary medals bear suspension loops and were presumably intended to be worn from ribbons or stitched onto uniform sashes or tunics.

An example of an early medal – the *Naval Reward of Charles II*, granted for distinguished service in the Dutch Wars. Following in the wake of the Commonwealth naval rewards, they could be seen as the beginning of a national system of such awards but in fact no such system developed in the eighteenth century.

It is highly likely that some of the varied medals awarded by local commanders during the Civil Wars of 1642–51 (see above, p. 12) were given specifically for gallantry in action, but the details are lost. Many would have been for meritorious, loyal or long service as much as for individual acts of gallantry.

Throughout the remainder of the seventeenth century no national system of awarding medals for gallantry developed, though the germ of such a system did indeed appear in the form of the *Commonwealth Naval Medals*. These were awarded from 1649 for 'extraordinary service' at sea or in the Dutch wars of the 1650s, but although their limited use continued into the reigns of Charles II (with the *Naval Rewards* of 1665) and William and Mary, a standardised system did not develop. Throughout the eighteenth century, there was a return to the more or less ad hoc awarding of medals to individuals (usually naval officers) for distinguished or gallant service, the medals being authorised by Act of Parliament, by Royal Warrant or even by societies or individuals to reward outstanding service. Since they were produced by so many different agencies, they vary enormously in size and design and few seem to have been conferred on lower ranks or in any number.

There are many examples of these individual or limited awards. One is the *Callis Gold Medal and Chain* awarded by King George II to Captain Smith Callis who destroyed five Spanish ships at St Tropez in June 1742. Silver medals were given to officers commanding other British ships engaged – but nothing to the lower ranks. Even the major campaigns of the later eighteenth century sparked no national system of awards. There are very few known medals for the Seven Years War of 1756–63 and fewer still for the American campaigns of the Revolutionary War of 1776–83.

But there was a growing feeling, at least on the part of unit and regimental commanders, that something ought to be done to reward the gallantry of their own men. The absence of any official system to recognise gallantry in battle regardless of rank really began to be felt during the long French Revolutionary and Napoleonic Wars of 1793–1815. Britain's armies and navies were committed around the world on a much larger scale than in some of the major wars of the eighteenth century and the war dragged on far longer than any other. Acts of gallantry by British land forces – for example, in Portugal, Spain or Egypt – and by her naval forces around the globe were frequently reported and clearly merited some form of recognition. The result was the proliferation of 'unofficial' regimental medals for merit, gallantry or distinguished service on a scale never before seen. The majority were created and conferred by regimental commanders or groups of officers, clearly anxious to give formal recognition to the

An example of an unofficial regimental award for gallantry during the Peninsular War, in this case to a soldier of the 1st 43rd Light Infantry, 1814. Since there were no official awards for gallantry, many regiments produced their own types, often in silver and entirely engraved, like this one.

gallantry of their men. Many regiments created their own awards and the evidence suggests that they were worn in uniform and were highly regarded. If nothing else, they provided some form of morale booster for the rest of the men who could see that their bravery in action might be recognised and the reward made publicly visible. (For a detailed survey, see *Regimental and Volunteer Medals, 1745–1895*, Vol. I, J L Balmer: (Loughborough, Langlands, 1988).)

It could be claimed that the *Navy Gold Medals* (1793–1815) and their Army equivalents, the *Army Gold Crosses* and *Army Gold Medals* created during the French Wars, mark the beginning of a standardised system of recognition. Although some were indeed conferred for bravery in action or leadership under fire, many were equally awarded for 'distinguished' rather than specifically 'gallant' service or for leadership on campaign. And since they were only granted to officers and ceased to be awarded after 1815, they do not actually represent the beginning of a national system of rewards. Similarly, the extension of the existing *Order of the Bath* in 1815 did produce another available reward – the new lower-tier *Companion of the Order of the Bath* (CB). It was originally intended to reward lower ranking officers for distinguished service during the French Wars and some continued to be conferred for gallantry late into the nineteenth century. But the CB increasingly became an officers' reward for long and/or distinguished service, frequently conferred upon retirement and was only rarely granted for specific acts of gallantry.

The Role of the East India Company

As with the introduction of standardised
campaign medals, it was the EIC that took the
first step towards establishing a formalised
system of gallantry awards when in 1837 it
instituted the *Order of Merit*. In three classes (a solid-gold 1st
Class, a gold and silver 2nd Class and a silver 3rd Class), the
Order was conferred only for personal gallantry in action and
was only awarded to Indian soldiers – not to their
British officers or to British forces serving alongside
EIC units. Recipients received increased pay and
pensions and posthumous awards were allowed, in
which case the pension went to the recipient's
widow, if he had one. The award was highly
regarded and remained the only gallantry medal
available to Indian soldiers up to 1907, when the
Indian Distinguished Service Medal (IDSM) was
introduced as a 'lower level' gallantry award.

Regarded as the 'Indian VC', the Order became
known as the *Indian Order of Merit* (IOM) in 1902 to distinguish it
from the British *Order of Merit* (OM) established in that year. Although
Indian soldiers became eligible for the Victoria Cross in 1911, the IOM
remained in use, but was then reduced to two classes and to one in 1944.
When India became independent in 1947 the IOM was rendered obsolete,
along with other specifically British-Indian awards like the IDSM.

The Effects of the Russian War, 1854–56

As late as the middle of the nineteenth century, Britain still had no national
system of rewarding all ranks of her armed forces for gallantry in action.
This situation only changed as a direct result of the Russian War of 1854–56.
Britain, in alliance with the Ottoman Empire, France and later Sardinia,
declared war on Russia in 1854 to defend Turkish integrity and prevent
Russian expansion into the strategically vital eastern Mediterranean. As
usual with Britain's involvement in a large-scale European war, her
contribution was largely to have been naval – and British fleets did indeed
operate in the Baltic, the Black Sea and Sea of Azoff, the White Sea and the
Pacific. But the war is remembered today not so much for Britain's naval
commitment as for her land operations on the Crimean peninsula and in the
siege of the Russian naval base of Sebastopol. The Crimean War was, more

Above: The *Indian Order of Merit*: the first official gallantry award. This is the 2nd Class,
which has a central gold wreath, of 1837–1912.

importantly, reported in detail by what were effectively the first real war correspondents, such as W H Russell of *The Times*. These men reported the incidents of the war against Russia and brought before the British public the real state of affairs in the Crimea – the losses in battle, the inefficiency of the Army, the poor food and desperately bad medical arrangements, which all contributed to the suffering of the soldiers on active service.

The greater awareness of the nature of the fighting led to calls for the establishment of a proper system for rewarding gallantry and finally a new system of decorations was created. The first was the *Distinguished Conduct Medal* (DCM), instituted in December 1854 for the Other Ranks of the Army. Its counterpart for the Other Ranks of the Royal Navy and Royal Marines was the *Conspicuous Gallantry Medal* (CGM), instituted in September 1855. Only ten of the latter were actually awarded for the Crimean War and the medal effectively lapsed until formally revived in 1874 as a result of the Ashanti War.

Above: The obverse of the *Distinguished Conduct Medal* (DCM), 1854–1901. The medal is somewhat unusual in not displaying the effigy of the monarch (until 1901) and has the same reverse by Benedetto Pistrucci used on the *Army Long Service and Good Conduct Medal* until 1901.

Below: The *Conspicuous Gallantry Medal* (CGM); Victorian issue as revived in 1874.

Both medals carried financial rewards in the form of pensions or gratuities and were highly regarded from the outset. Some 800 DCMs were conferred for the Crimean War and they continued to be awarded up until the reform of the honours' system in 1993. In many of the smaller colonial wars, the DCM was sparingly awarded, so that examples are rare for some campaigns; examples are Indian Mutiny (only approximately 18 known), Abyssinia 1867–68 (7), Ashanti 1873–74 (33), South Africa 1877–79 (16), Afghanistan 1878–80 (61), Egypt 1882–89 (134). Compare this with the approximately 25,000 awarded for 1914–18. The DCM fell victim to the reforms of 1993 when it was rendered obsolete, along with most other medals (as opposed to crosses) for gallantry.

The Victoria Cross

The creation of the DCM and the CGM at last produced a standardised system of rewards for gallant conduct on campaign but neither of these could be awarded to officers. These still effectively had no gallantry award open to them, unless one includes the *Order of the Bath* at Companion level (CB), which was rarely conferred for bravery on campaign as opposed to 'distinguished service' over a longer period. Demands for a more comprehensive awards' system continued to be made in Parliament and in the press while the Crimean War was being fought. The result, with the active support of the Queen and the Prince Consort, was the institution of the *Victoria Cross* in January 1856, made retrospective to the beginning of the Russian War in October 1854. It was, for its time, a remarkably democratic award, being open in the same form to all ranks and to all arms of the British service. There were no separate 'classes' as there were with the older Orders and no distinction between awards to officers and Other Ranks. The plain simplicity of design of the bronze cross caused some adverse comment at the time, but the deliberate intention was to create an award that was valued for what it represented – 'Valour', as on the Cross – and not for any decorative element. For the naval and land campaigns against Russia, 1854–56, 111 VCs were awarded with no fewer than 62 being personally presented by the Queen at a grand review in Hyde Park in June 1857 – the first time that such an award parade had been held and the first view of the new VC. Its award was extended gradually to civilians (prior to 1881), to the Indian army (in 1911) and to air forces and Merchant Navy

Above: The *Victoria Cross*. Until 1918, the ribbon on Army awards (as here) was dark red and for RN and RM service dark blue. The ribbon was standardised to dark red in 1918.

personnel as the dictates of twentieth-century warfare war decreed. The *Victoria Cross* remains Britain's highest award for gallantry 'before the enemy' – and one of the most highly regarded in the world. At the time of writing, 1,356 have been conferred, the most recent for current operations in Iraq and Afghanistan.

The Development of Gallantry Awards

Military Awards

By 1914, there existed a range of military rewards for gallantry in battle. The *Victoria Cross* (VC), the *Distinguished Conduct Medal* (DCM) and its naval equivalent the *Conspicuous Gallantry Medal* (CGM), all dating from the Crimean War, continued to be awarded after 1856. In addition, the *Distinguished Service Order* (DSO) was created in 1886 to reward junior officers on campaign. Although styled as an 'Order' whose recipients were 'admitted' to it, the DSO had only one class and was only conferred on officers for military (not civilian) service and is really a decoration rather than a true Order. While some were undoubtedly conferred for personal gallantry in action (e.g in Burma 1885–87), many were for more generally defined 'distinguished' or meritorious service during a particular campaign and some were awarded for administrative and non-combat duties. This aspect rankled so much during the First World War – when the DSO was frequently awarded for work far behind the fighting lines – that in January 1917 it was decreed that the decoration would only be granted to 'fighting services', the implication being that it would only go to those who had distinguished themselves 'in the face of the

Above right: The reverse of the *Victorian Distinguished Service Order* (DSO), with the monarch's cypher, 'VRI'. The earliest awards, 1886–89, were worked in gold and enamels, after which they were produced in silver-gilt. The reverse always shows the current cypher of the reigning monarch.

Left: The Victorian DSO in gold (as awarded 1886–89) with campaign medal for Egypt and its associated *Khedive's Star*, dated '1884–86'. The obverse of the DSO (shown) has remained the same since 1886, with only slight variations in the detail of the crown.

enemy'. Since 1993, the DSO has been opened to all ranks but has lost its status as a gallantry award, now being granted for qualities of leadership.

The last gallantry award created before the First World War was the rarely conferred *Conspicuous Service Cross* (CSC). Instituted in 1901, it was intended to reward junior officers of the Royal Navy for gallantry on campaign. Only eight had been conferred prior to 1914, so examples are very rare, and it was effectively superseded by the *Distinguished Service Cross* (DSC) in 1914 (see below).

The severity of the day-to-day fighting on land and sea in 1914–15 quickly brought to the fore the need for a wider range of decorations for bravery. The many acts of gallantry being performed in all theatres necessitated the creation of new awards to meet the novel circumstances of the First World War; the result was a plethora of new decorations, all of which were additionally granted to imperial forces, though not usually to the Other Ranks of the Indian army, which had its own established system of gallantry awards.

The first new officers' award was the *Distinguished Service Cross* (DSC), instituted on the 14 October 1914 (though largely a simple re-foundation of the *Conspicuous Gallantry Cross* of 1901) for junior officers and senior warrant officers of the Royal Navy. Next came the *Military Cross* (MC), established on the 28 December 1914, to recognise the gallantry 'in the field' of junior

The *Military Cross* with awards for the Second World War. The MC bears the cypher of the reigning monarch in the centre. Its reverse is plain, though after *c.* 1938 the year of award was engraved on the lower arms and it is often seen privately engraved with the recipient's details. Formerly (1914–93) an award for junior officers and senior NCOs, it was made available to all ranks in 1993.

officers and senior NCOs of the Army and air services where their actions fell short of the requirement for the DSO or (in the case of senior NCOs) above that which would earn the existing DCM. Approximately 3,000 DSCs and 40,000 MCs (including further award bars) were conferred for the First World War. For the Second World War, as for gallantry awards in general, the figures are much lower – approximately 4,500 and 11,500 respectively.

Since it was widely expected that Britain's role in a world war would be primarily as a naval power, the *Distinguished Service Medal* was authorised in October 1914 specifically as a lower level reward for the Other Ranks of the Royal Navy. Awarded for service afloat or on land, it was also conferred on the Royal Naval Air Service and in 1942 was extended to the men of the

Above: The *Distinguished Service Medal* (DSM) for 1914–18, with related campaign medals for the First World War (*1914–15 Star, British War Medal* and *Victory Medal*). The *Victory Medal* carries the *Mentioned in Dispatches* emblem (see p. 138). The King is shown in Admiral's uniform.

Left: Obverses of the *Distinguished Conduct Medal*, 1914–18 and the *Military Medal*. The DCM bears a second award bar of the laurelled type used on many British gallantry awards and as extra-service bars on long-service medals. Approximately 25,000 DCMs were awarded 1914–20 and approximately 116,000 MMs.

Royal Artillery (serving as gunners on defensively armed merchant ships (DAMS)), and on the Merchant Navy. Only 4,500 (including bars) were awarded for the First World War and approximately 7,200 for the Second World War – reflecting the more extensive and organised use of convoys.

This award to personnel of the Royal Navy was eventually mirrored by a new lower level award for the Army. The especially difficult conditions of trench warfare on the Western Front resulted in the creation in March 1916 of the *Military Medal* (MM), an award for the Other Ranks of the Army and some other services (e.g. the Royal Flying Corps, which at that time had no distinctive air awards). As with other decorations, additional bars could be awarded for further acts of gallantry. Over 125,000 MMs (including further award bars) were issued prior to 1920 and a further 15,500 for the Second World War, the award being extended to Indian soldiers in 1944 even though these continued to receive the *Indian Order of Merit* or *Indian Distinguished Service Medal*. The specifically Indian awards became obsolete in 1947 when India was granted independence.

Air combat was a novelty of the First World War and eventually included the use not only of fighter planes, but also spotter planes (for directing artillery), long-range heavy bombers, seaplanes, airships and kite balloons. At first, the gallantry displayed by aerial forces was rewarded with existing military or naval awards such as the VC and the DSO, as well as the MC, DCM and MM (for the Royal Flying Corps) and equivalent naval awards (like the DSC and DSM) for the Royal Naval Air Service. With the creation of a unified Royal Air Force in April 1918, it was at last decided to produce specific awards for the air services. The result was the creation of two combat awards – the *Distinguished Flying Cross* (DFC) for officers and the *Distinguished Flying Medal* (DFM) for Other Ranks. At the same time, two equivalent awards for gallantry or distinguished service not 'in the face of the enemy' were created – the *Air Force Cross* (AFC) for officers and the *Air Force Medal* (AFM) for Other Ranks. All four were instituted in June 1918. Given that these were created late in the war, they are not common for the

Above: The *Distinguished Flying Cross*. The RAF awards (DFC, AFC, DFM and AFM) are much more elaborate and decorative that their Army and Navy counterparts. The original award had a horizontal striped ribbon, soon altered to that now in use and seen here. The reverse is plain except for a central roundel bearing the cypher of George V (as founder) and the foundation date '1918'.

The ornate *Air Force Cross*, introduced in 1918 for non-combatant gallantry with aerial forces. It is seen here with campaign stars and the *War Medal* for 1939–45.

First World War but were much more frequently awarded for the Second World War, when air combat and air bombing played a much greater roll in the general conduct of the war. For 1939–45, for example, no fewer than 22,000 DFCs or additional bars were conferred. Today, the Crosses (DFC and AFC) remain in use – now available to all ranks – but the medals (DFM and AFM) fell victim to the reforms of 1993 and are no longer awarded.

The lowest form of 'wearable' award is the *Mentioned in Dispatches* emblem. Prior to the First World War, officers (in particular) and soldiers or sailors had frequently been 'mentioned in dispatches' by senior officers for gallant, distinguished or meritorious service on campaign. Apart from promotions resulting from this recognition (e.g. brevet or advanced promotion for officers), there was no visible emblem to show that a person had been 'MID' until 1919. The sheer numbers of service personnel who had had their names 'brought forward' for noteworthy service forced a change to the system. In 1919 it was decreed that anyone who was officially 'mentioned' for service during the First World War (though the opportunity was not taken to make the system retrospective any earlier than August 1914) would wear an emblem in the form of a bronze oak-leaf spray on the *Victory Medal* (if awarded). Only one emblem could be worn, no matter how many times the recipient had been 'mentioned'. In August 1920, the emblem was altered to a single bronze oak-leaf emblem, worn on the ribbon of the appropriate campaign medal (only the *War Medal* in the case of Second World War awards), and in 1993 the emblem was changed from bronze to silver. It is still conferred and all recipients are listed in the *London Gazette*, as with other official awards.

The latest award for gallantry is the *Conspicuous Gallantry Cross*, instituted as a result of the reforms of 1993 with the intention of reducing the number of decorations available and in particular to remove the distinctions in rank associated with gallantry awards. It was intended as a high-level gallantry award, ranking just below the VC, and its creation rendered obsolete the DCM, the CGM and the DSO (as awarded for gallantry). The first awards were made in 1995 for service in Bosnia.

It should be noted that all military gallantry medals (as opposed to crosses) became obsolete in 1993 on the reorganisation of the honours' system under Prime Minister John Major. However, the predominantly civilian awards, the *George Medal* (1940) and the *Queen's Gallantry Medal* (1974) (q.v.) may still be conferred on service personnel.

Top right: The oak-leaf spray worn to show a 'mention in dispatches' between 1914 and 1920.

Above right: The bronze *Mentioned in Dispatches* oak-leaf emblem, used between 1920 and 1993. Now awarded in silver.

Above left: The *Conspicuous Gallantry Cross*, a new high-level gallantry award, second only to the *Victoria Cross*. Instituted in 1993 and first awarded for Bosnia, 1995, it effectively replaced the DSO (for gallantry), the DCM and the CGM. The reverse is plain.

Civilian Gallantry

As with military rewards for gallantry, official medals for civilian bravery were only slowly established. In fact, awards for bravery in saving life were, in their earliest days, very much the province of specialist life-saving societies, private organisations or even individuals and were produced throughout the country from the late eighteenth century onwards. Even after the official issue of such awards (like the *Sea Gallantry Medal* of 1855, the *Albert Medal* of 1866 or the *Edward Medal* of 1909), local and national societies continued to play a major role in recognising gallantry in saving life – or simply attempting to save life – on land and sea. Some, like the Royal Humane Society and RNLI, continue to do so to the present day.

These medals are keenly collected, often for their local interest and because the circumstances of the awards are researchable in official records, the appropriate society reports and in local newspapers. Examples of local societies that rewarded bravery in the saving of life are the Hundred of Salford Humane Society and the Liverpool Shipwreck and Humane Society, both of which issued medals for various types of incident. The Hundred of Salford Humane Society was one of many founded in Britain as an offshoot of the Royal Humane Society. It was established in 1789 and revived in 1824 and awarded medals until 1922 for bravery in saving life specifically in the Salford and Manchester areas. The Liverpool Shipwreck and Humane Society was another of the many formed throughout Britain in the nineteenth century to reward gallantry in saving life in a variety of circumstances. Established in 1839, it was originally set up to administer a fund to reward those who had suffered from or had rendered aid during a storm in the Irish Channel in January 1839. It issued a variety of attractive medals for saving life at sea, on land or from fire. The first awards were large and not intended for wear, but were replaced in about 1871 with a wearable oval silver medal bearing on one side the words 'Liverpool Shipwreck and Humane Society 1839' surrounding a scene showing a shipwrecked mariner on a raft, lifting a drowning child from the sea. Above were the words 'Lord save us we perish'. The medal hung from an attractive suspension formed

Above: The *Liverpool Shipwreck and Humane Society's Marine Medal* in silver, third type, post-1867. One of a range of well-produced medals awarded by the Society in gold, silver or bronze for gallantry in saving life under different circumstances. The reverse of this type shows the famous Liver Bird surrounded by a wreath.

from the Liver Bird motif of the city of Liverpool. The medal was altered in 1867 to a more standardised circular silver medal of 38mm, issued in gold, silver and bronze, with a swivelling scroll suspension and engraved with the recipient's details around the edge. Plain bars bearing the date of the award were conferred for further acts of gallantry. Another of this society's awards was the Society's *Fire Medal*. First conferred in 1883, it was awarded in gold, silver and bronze for bravery in saving life from fire. The medal bore on the obverse a scene of a fireman carrying children from a burning house and delivering them into the arms of their mother.

One other example of these active societies is the Shipwrecked Fishermen and Mariners Royal Benevolent Society, founded in 1839 to provide aid to shipwrecked mariners and to the dependants of those lost at sea. It issued gold and silver medals from 1851 for 'heroic or praiseworthy exertions to save life from shipwreck etc.'. The medals were engraved around the edge with the recipient's name and the date of award.

The first national society to make medallic awards for gallantry in saving life was the Humane Society (later Royal Humane Society), originally founded in 1774 to teach life saving and emergency resuscitation – hence the obverse design on its medals. It was originally only concerned with the rescue of those who risked drowning or with rescues at sea and initially awarded large non-wearable or 'table' medals in gold, silver and bronze, as well as monetary rewards, certificates and practical gifts like binoculars to those who had saved life at sea or risked their own life in a rescue attempt.

The medals depicted on their obverse a cherub blowing on a glowing ember and the words '*lateat scintillvla forsan*' ('lest a small spark be hidden') – a reference to resuscitation – with a three-line text in the exergue, with the society's title in abbreviated Latin and the date of foundation in Roman numerals, 'mdcclxxiv'. The reverse had a wreath of oak leaves with details of the recipient and action engraved in the centre, around which is the Latin legend '*hoc pretivm cive servato tvlit*' ('he has obtained this reward for saving the life of a citizen'). When awarded for an unsuccessful rescue attempt, this

Above: The Royal Humane Society medal in bronze, post-1869, when the medal was reduced to become a wearable award. With integral bronze wearing brooch. The gallantry medals are still awarded by the RHS in silver or bronze.

wording was omitted. Since they were not intended to be worn, the medals of 1774–1869 had no ribbon or suspension.

The Society later broadened its remit to include rescue attempts of all kinds, including mining, industry, transport etc. and in the military as well as civil spheres and in 1869 was granted permission for its medals to be worn in uniform, though on the right breast, not the left as with official awards. Their size was reduced to the standard 38mm diameter, suspended from a plain dark-blue ribbon via the usual swivelling scroll suspension. At the same time, the reverse inscriptions were altered to reflect successful or unsuccessful attempts. The former bore *'vit. ob. serv. d.d. soc. reg. hvm'* '('the Royal Humane Society presented this gift for saving life'), while the latter bore *'vit. peric. expos. d.d. soc. reg. hvm'* ('the Royal Humane Society presented this gift, his life having been exposed to peril'). They were engraved around the rim with the recipient's details and the date of the action. Subsequent acts were rewarded by clasps of the appropriate metal with 'RHS' and the engraved date of the incident. From 1873, a gold medal (in memory of Captain C S S Stanhope) was awarded to the rescue deemed to be the most gallant of the year. At first, it resembled the RHS silver award, but in gold and with clasp reading 'Stanhope Medal' below the year of award (e.g. '1896'). However, since 1937 the *Stanhope Medal* has been identical to the other RHS medals, except that it is worked in gold. The RHS medals and certificates are still awarded.

The earliest national system specifically for saving life at sea or in shipwrecks was established by what is now the Royal National Lifeboat Institution. Founded on 4 March 1824 as the Royal National Institution for the Preservation of Life from Shipwreck and as the RNLI from 1854, it awarded medals in gold and silver from 1825 and from 1917 in bronze. They are conferred upon 'persons whose humane and intrepid exertions in saving life from shipwreck on our coasts are deemed sufficiently conspicuous to

merit honourable distinction'. Since 1825 five different obverse and two reverse types have been issued and the medals are still awarded, mainly to lifeboat personnel who risk their lives in rescue attempts.

Left: The *Board of Trade Medal for Gallantry* or *Sea Gallantry Medal*. Edward VII issue. Medals in gold, silver or bronze were awarded from 1855. The awards, previously larger and without suspension, were reduced to a wearable medal in 1903.

The first official medal awarded for saving life was the Board of Trade's *Sea Gallantry Medal*. It originated with the Merchant Shipping Act of 1854 which made provision for rewards for bravery in saving life at sea; it is the only award for gallantry instituted by Act of Parliament. The original award was a large bronze 'table medal' of 58mm diameter, not intended for wear. Its reverse bore a striking scene of a group of men, women and children tending a shipwrecked sailor awaiting rescue. Provision was made for gold, silver and bronze medals, but no gold medal is known. The silver and bronze types were issued with one of two obverse legends surrounding the monarch's profile – an award for gallantry with 'Awarded by the Board of Trade for Gallantry in Saving Life' or a medal for 'humanity' with the legend 'Awarded by the Board of Trade for Saving Life at Sea'. The gallantry award was made to those who risked their lives in attempting a rescue, while the other was conferred on those who provided support services at a rescue, such as a ship's captain. The 'humanity' medal was rarely awarded, the last being issued in 1893.

In 1904, the award was brought into line with other British gallantry medals by being reduced to a smaller, wearable medal of 33mm. Again, there were two types. The first obverse of 1904–5 had 'awarded by the Board of Trade for gallantry in saving life at sea' around the King's profile; the second type of 1905–10 bore the simpler legend 'for gallantry in saving life at sea' around the King's profile. The ribbon is red with two narrow white stripes.

The prestigious and high-ranking *Albert Medal*, named in memory of Albert, the Prince Consort (d. 1861) and instituted by Royal Warrant in March 1866, originally had only one class and was initially awarded only to recognise gallantry in saving life at sea. Within a year, it was extended to two classes, known as the *Albert Medal of the First Class* and the *Albert Medal of the Second Class*. In 1877, the award was extended to life saving on land. It became a highly esteemed decoration, sometimes referred to as the 'civilian VC', but it could also be awarded to military personnel for acts of gallantry not 'before the enemy' (e.g. dealing with fires at ammunition stores). The medal's title was changed again in 1917, the First

Above: The *Albert Medal* in bronze, for land service. The land medal had a red enamel centre and red and white ribbon, while the sea-service version had blue enamel and a blue and white ribbon.

Class becoming the *Albert Medal in Gold* and the bronze Second Class simply the *Albert Medal*. The medal for service at sea has the words 'For Gallantry in Saving Life at Sea' around a central blue enamelled plaque, in which are the intertwined initials of Victoria and Albert. It was worn from a blue and white ribbon. The medal for land service bore the legend 'For Gallantry in Saving Life on Land' around a red enamelled centre, again with intertwined V and A. Its ribbon was crimson and white.

In 1949, the medal in gold was abolished, being replaced by the new *George Cross* (q.v.) and the second-class medal became solely a posthumous award. Since the larger number of available gallantry medals was causing some confusion as to requirements for award, in 1971 the *Albert Medal* ceased to be conferred altogether and all living recipients were allowed to exchange their award for the *George Cross* – though not all chose to do so.

In 1907 a new award, the *Edward Medal*, was instituted to recognise civilian acts of gallantry at a level lower than that necessary to earn the *Albert Medal*. As first instituted, it was to reward bravery in saving life in mines and quarries, but in 1909 a second type was added for similar service in any industrial context. The two medals bore different reverses. That for quarries and mines depicted a rescuer coming to the aid of a miner trapped underground, while that for industry showed a rescuer supporting a fallen workman in a collapsing building, below the words 'For Courage'.

The reverse of the medal 'for industry' was altered in 1912 to a more symbolic design, with a standing female figure holding a laurel spray, with the words 'For Courage' on either side. Both medals were awarded in silver and bronze, originally designated the *Edward Medal 1st Class* and the *Edward Medal 2nd Class* but in 1917, the titles were altered to the *Edward Medal in Gold* and the *Edward Medal in Silver*.

With the institution of the *George Cross* and *George Medal* in 1940, the rewarding of civilian gallantry became somewhat confused. As a result, it was decreed in 1949 that, like the *Albert Medal*, awards of the silver *Edward Medal* should cease and that the bronze medal should only be awarded posthumously. In 1971, again like the *Albert Medal*, the award of the *Edward Medal* ceased and living recipients were allowed to exchange their medal for

Above: One of the rarest gallantry awards: the *Edward Medal* (1907). This is the second class, in bronze, with reverse for mine or quarry rescues.

the *George Cross*. Approximately 77 silver and 318 bronze for mines and 25 silver and 163 bronze for industry were awarded.

For other services in which lives may have been put at risk in executing rescues, other specific awards were introduced. The *King's Police Medal* (1909–54) was instituted in July 1909, to reward police and fire-service personnel in Britain and dominions for gallant or distinguished service. The reverse bore a standing helmeted figure, with a sword and shield, the latter bearing the words 'To Guard My People'. Prior to 1933, there was no distinction between those awarded for gallantry and those for distinguished service, but in that year, two reverse types were introduced, with 'For Gallantry' or 'For Distinguished Service' in the reverse exergue. Dated bars were authorised for additional service but from 1934, these were altered to the usual laurel design. The original ribbon was blue with silver edges. A silver central stripe was introduced in 1916 and in 1933, when the two distinct versions were authorised, gallantry awards added an additional thin red stripe bisecting the silver stripes.

In 1940, to recognise the exertions of the fire-fighting services during the Blitz and other air attacks, the medal was officially re-designated the *King's Police and Fire Brigade Medal*, though its design remained the same. In 1950, it was decreed that the 'gallantry' version would only be awarded posthumously and in 1954 the award was entirely discontinued, with separate medals being instituted for the police and fire services (see below).

The *Queen's Police Medal* was instituted in May 1954, to replace the above award for police service. The reverse design retains that of the earlier KPM and also has two reverses, with 'For Distinguished Police Service' or 'For Gallantry' inscribed around the circumference. The posthumous award for gallantry effectively became redundant in 1977 when the *George Medal* was made available to the police.

At the same time, May 1954, to separate police and fire-service awards the *Queen's Fire Service Medal* was created. The reverse design retains that of the earlier KPM and equally has two possible reverses, with 'For Distinguished Fire Service' or 'For Gallantry' inscribed around the circumference. The ribbon is yellow with two wide red stripes for the distinguished service type, while the gallantry version has narrow red stripes bisecting the yellow stripes. As with the *Queen's Police Medal*, posthumous awards for gallantry became redundant in 1977 when the *George Medal* was made available to the fire services.

A wider ranging civilian award was the *Medal of the Order of the British Empire* (1917–22), instituted in 1917 as a lower tier of the newly established *Order of the British Empire*. The small silver medal was originally worn from a plain purple ribbon but in December 1918 a military division was created, distinguished by the addition of a narrow central red stripe through the ribbon. Regrettably, these medals were issued unnamed, though examples are seen privately engraved, and it is not easy to locate information on the deeds for which they were awarded. Only approximately 2,000 were issued before the medal was superseded in 1922 by the *British Empire Medal* (see below).

A specific version for gallantry, the *Medal of the Order of the British Empire for Gallantry*, commonly referred to as the *Empire Gallantry Medal* (EGM), was instituted in December 1922, together with the *British Empire Medal* for meritorious service, both replacing the medal introduced in 1917. They are unusual in that they do not bear the effigy and titles of the reigning monarch. The EGM had both civil and military divisions, distinguished only by the ribbon, and was awarded for specific acts of gallantry, though not usually 'before the enemy'. It bore the words 'For Gallantry' and a suspension ornamented with laurel leaves. When the Order was reorganised in 1937, the ribbon was altered to pink with pearl-grey edges (for civil awards), military awards having an additional narrow central stripe of pearl grey.

Because there was little visible difference in the gallantry and 'meritorious' awards of the *British Empire Medal*, it was decided in 1933 to add a small silver laurel-branch emblem which would be worn on the ribbon of the gallantry award as a visual distinction. In 1940, the EGM was superseded by the *George Cross* (see below) and recipients were asked to exchange their awards. Not all, however, agreed to do so and retained their original award. Only 130 were awarded before 1940, 64 for civil actions, 62 to military recipients and 4 honorary. To confuse matters further, the standard BEM continued to be awarded in certain circumstances for gallantry and to distinguish these from awards for 'meritorious' service, two small crossed oak leaves in silver were worn on the BEM ribbon from 1954–74, when the Queen's Gallantry Medal was introduced.

The circumstances of the Second World War – with its unprecedented attack on civilian populations – led to the creation of two new gallantry awards, the *George Cross* and the *George Medal* (both instituted in September 1940). Although they were really intended to reward civilian gallantry or gallantry not 'in a theatre of war',

The *George Cross*, obverse, with the image of St George and the dragon.

they were also conferred on military personnel but, as with the *Albert Medal*, for actions other than under enemy fire (e.g. saving lives on minefields etc.) and in circumstances where purely military awards may not have been appropriate. The most unusual awards are those to the island of Malta in 1942, which honoured the population as a whole for their gallantry in defence of the island, and that recently conferred as a unit award on the Royal Ulster Constabulary.

The highest civilian award for gallantry, the *George Cross*, is granted 'only for acts of the greatest heroism or of the most conspicuous courage in circumstances of extreme danger'. Fewer than 170 have been conferred, excluding exchanges of the *Empire Gallantry Medal* and most recent awards have been posthumous. The decoration takes the form of a plain Greek cross in silver, with a central medallion depicting St George and the Dragon, around which is the legend 'For Gallantry'. The angle of each arm of the Cross carries the royal cypher 'G.VI'. The reverse is plain and bears the recipient's name and date of the award (not the date of the deed for which the award is made).

The *George Medal*, instituted at the same time as the *George Cross* but for a lower level of gallantry, essentially rewards 'acts of great bravery' and ranks next below the *George Cross*. As with the *George Cross*, awards have been made to military personnel for actions not under enemy fire or where purely military awards were not appropriate and to foreign recipients. Approximately 2,000 medals and 25 bars have been conferred, about half of which were given to military recipients. The circular silver medal bears on the obverse the usual effigy and titles of the monarch, while the reverse carries a figure of St George slaying the Dragon, with the words 'The George Medal'. Further award bars were authorised in the original Warrant. No recipient has received two bars. The ribbon is red with five equidistant narrow blue stripes and as with the *George Cross* and other awards, female recipients wear the medal from a bow fashioned from the medal ribbon.

The most recent addition to the range of civilian gallantry awards is the *Queen's Gallantry Medal*, which was instituted in June 1974 to recognise acts of gallantry by the emergency services and civilians, though forces' personnel can receive the

The reverse of the *Queen's Gallantry Medal* (QGM), an award for civilian or military gallantry introduced in 1974. It effectively replaced any awards within the Order of the British Empire for gallantry.

award for gallantry in circumstances where military awards are not appropriate. With its introduction, the award of the BEM for gallantry (q.v.) ceased. Citizens of both Britain and Commonwealth are eligible. The obverse bears the effigy and titles of the monarch, while the rather plain reverse simply has the 'Queen's Gallantry Medal' below a crown, with a spray of laurel on either side. The silver medal is impressed with the recipient's details around the edge and a bar may be awarded for further acts of gallantry.

Principal Awards for Gallantry, 1854–2008

All official British awards are notified/published in the *London Gazette*. For a detailed study, see *British Gallantry Awards*, P E Abbott and J M A Tamplin (revised 2nd edn, London, Nimrod Dix & Co., 1981). For a good overview of military and many civilian awards prior to 1940, see *Gallantry*, Sir A Wilson and J H F McEwen (London, 1939; reprinted Oxford, OUP, 1980). The following useful guides, which may be read online or downloaded, are available online from TNA:

Medals: British Armed Services, Gallantry
Medals: British Armed Services, Gallantry, Further Information
Merchant Seamen: Medals and Honours.

The Victoria Cross, 1856–to date

Instituted by Royal Warrant of 29 January 1856 and announced in the *London Gazette* 5 February 1856, its first awards were published on 24 February 1857. Up to the time of writing, 1,356 have been awarded. The literature on the VC is very large and continues to grow. Basic introductions and listings are in:

- *The Evolution of the Victoria Cross*, M J Crook (Tunbridge Wells, Midas Books, 1976)
- *The Victoria Cross*, P Duckers (Oxford, Shire, 2005)
- *Symbol of Courage: A Complete History of the Victoria Cross*, M Arthur (London, Sidgwick & Jackson, 2003)
- *The Register of the Victoria Cross* (Cheltenham, This England, 1988).

For a detailed bibliography, the reader is recommended to consult *Victoria Cross Bibliography*, J Mulholland and A Jordan (eds) (London, Spink, 1999).
    Files on the VC are held at TNA under series WO.98.

The New Zealand Cross, 1869

Instituted by the New Zealand government during the 2nd Maori War (1860–72), this was intended to reward the gallantry of the local militia which bore the brunt of the fighting but for whom the VC was not then available. Its institution led to a severe rebuke to the Governor, who had no authority to create such decorations, but the Queen eventually sanctioned the award. However, the Cross was effectively rendered obsolete by the end of the Maori Wars, the disbandment of most of the local war-raised forces and the extension of the VC to local colonial forces. Although still being conferred retrospectively as late as 1910, only twenty-three were ever granted, making this one of the rarest gallantry awards.

The Conspicuous Gallantry Cross, 1993–to date

The CGC was instituted as a high-level award in October 1993 in a series of reforms aimed at reducing the number of decorations available and in particular to remove the distinctions in rank associated with gallantry awards. The DCM, the CGM and the DSO (for gallantry) became obsolete as a result. The first awards were made in 1995 for service in Bosnia. (See photograph on p. 138.)

The George Cross, 1940–to date

Both the *George Cross* and the *George Medal* (q.v.) were instituted by Royal Warrant of 24 September 1940 (*London Gazette*, 31 January 1941) primarily to reward civilian gallantry at the highest level, though they could also be conferred on military personnel. Fewer than 170 have been granted, excluding exchanges of the *Empire Gallantry Medal* (q.v.). Since 1965, an annual pension (originally £100 per annum) has been paid to recipients. (See photograph on p. 145.)

- *The George Cross Register* (Cheltenham, This England, 1990)
- *The George Cross*, Ian Bisset (London, MacGibbon & Kee, 1961)
- *The Story of the George Cross*, Sir J Smyth (London, 1968)
- *The Register of the George Cross*, F G Carroll (Cheltenham, 1985)
- *One Step Further: those whose Gallantry was rewarded with the George Cross*, M Hebblethwaite (n.p., Chameleon, 2006)
- *Awards of the George Cross*, 1940–2005, J F Turner (Barnsley, Pen and Sword, 2006).

The Distinguished Service Order, 1886–to date

The DSO was instituted by Royal Warrant of 6 September 1886 to provide a form of immediate award for junior officers on campaign and for which existing awards available to officers (e.g. the CB) were not deemed appropriate. Rendered obsolete as an award for gallantry in 1993 with the introduction of the *Conspicuous Gallantry Cross* (q.v.), it was retained as an award 'for leadership' and is now open to all ranks. The first such appointments were made for service in operations in former Yugoslavia and Bosnia. (See photograph on p. 133.)

Award details:

- WO.390 (to 1945)
- WO.389 has a useful annotated 'pre-*Gazette*' listing which often adds detail
- *The DSO*, Sir O'M Creagh and E M Humphris (reprint, London, Hayward, 1978): awards up to 1926.

The Indian Order of Merit, 1837–1947

A gallantry award in three classes, the *Indian Order of Merit* was instituted by the East India Company in 1837, along with the *Order of British India* (q.v.). It was the first formally organised gallantry award and remained the only such award for native soldiers of the Indian army until the introduction of the *Indian Distinguished Service Medal* in 1907 (q.v.) and the extension of the *Victoria Cross* to Indian soldiers in 1911. (See photograph on p. 130.)

- *Deeds of Valour of the Indian Soldier which won the Indian Order of Merit*, P P Hypher, 2 Vols (1837–59 and 1859–1922) (Simla, 1921 and 1925)
- *Reward of Valor: the Indian Order of Merit, 1914–18*, P Duckers (n.p., Jade, 1999)
- *Unparalleled Danger, Unparalleled Courage: the Indian Order of Merit in the Second World War*, C Peterson (USA, Bookcrafters, 1997).

Conspicuous Service Cross, 1901

Instituted in June 1901, the *Conspicuous Service Cross* was intended as a gallantry award for junior commissioned officers and warrant officers of the Royal Navy. Only eight were awarded before 1910, so it is very rare. In October 1914, it was re-designated the *Distinguished Service Cross* (see below).

- see in *The Distinguished Service Cross, 1901–38*, W H Fevyer (Polstead, Hayward, 1991).

The Distinguished Service Cross, 1914–to date

The DSC originated in 1901 as the *Conspicuous Gallantry Cross* (q.v.) and was intended as an award for junior commissioned officers (below rank of Lieutenant Commander) and warrant officers of the Royal Navy for 'meritorious or distinguished services in action'. By Order in Council of 14 October 1914, the CGC was re-designated as the *Distinguished Service*

Cross. The award was extended in 1931 to Merchant and Fishing Fleets, in 1940 to RAF personnel and in 1942 to Army personnel serving afloat. The DSC was made available to all ranks following the reforms of 1993, the DSM (q.v.) then being rendered obsolete.

- *The Distinguished Service Cross, 1901–38*, W H Fevyer (Polstead, Hayward, 1991)
- *The Fringes of the Fleet and the Distinguished Service Cross*, R C Witte (London, DNW, 1997).

The Military Cross, 1914–to date

Introduced by Royal Warrant of 28 December 1914 (*London Gazette*, 1 January 1915) at the outset of the First World War, it was to reward junior commissioned officers and warrant officers of the Army, 'for gallant

Top: The *Distinguished Service Cross* (DSC) for 1914–18 with associated campaign awards. The obverse (seen) bears the cypher of the reigning monarch; the reverse is plain, though from 1940 the date of award was engraved on the lower arm. They are sometimes found privately engraved with the recipient's details.

Right: The obverse of the *Military Cross* (MC). Introduced in 1914, the MC bears the cypher of the reigning monarch, in this case King George VI. The reverse is plain unless privately named by the recipient, though those issued after 1936 have the year of award engraved on the lower limb.

and distinguished services in action', along the lines of the *Distinguished Service Cross* for the Royal Navy. It could be granted not only to officers of the Army, including those of Colonial and Indian forces, but also to Royal Marines officers and a few were given to naval and Air Force officers at various dates. Since 1993, it has been open to all ranks for gallantry.

Award details:

- WO.389 (to 1982). Indexed
- WO.389 has a useful annotated 'pre-*Gazette*' listing which often adds detail
- The *London Gazette* published some citations for 1914–18.

Note that New Year's Honours (January) and Birthday Honours (June) for 1914–18 were usually for generally good or meritorious service and do not have published citations.

- *Recipients of Bars to the Military Cross, 1916–1920*, J V Webb (privately published, 1988).
- *The Military Cross awarded to Officers and Warrant Officers, 1937–93*, R M Kamaryc (Harlow, 1993).

The Distinguished Flying Cross, 1918–to date

Instituted by Royal Warrant and *London Gazette* of 3 June 1918, the DFC was intended to recognise 'an act or acts of valour, courage or devotion to duty performed whilst on active operations against the enemy' under the specific conditions experienced by air forces. Second award bars were authorised at the same time. From 1939, the date of award is engraved on the reverse of the bar and on the lower arm of the cross itself. Since 1993, it has been open to all ranks. (See photograph on p. 136.)

- *Royal Air Force Awards 1918–19*, K J Nelson (n.p., 2001)
- *The Distinguished Flying Cross and how it was won, 1918–45*, N and C Carter (London, Savannah, 1998).

The Air Force Cross, 1918–to date

The AFC was introduced as a non-combatant equivalent of the DFC, being granted 'for exceptional valour, courage or devotion to duty whilst flying, though not in active operations against the enemy' (e.g. to test pilots, transport, air-sea rescue etc.) or for especially meritorious service. Like the DFC, it was instituted by Royal Warrant and *London Gazette* of 3 June 1918 and could be conferred upon commissioned officers and warrant officers of the RAF, the Fleet Air Arm, the Royal Navy and Colonial air forces. Since 1993, it is available to all ranks. (See photograph on p. 137.)

- *Royal Air Force Awards 1918–19*, K J Nelson (n.p., 2001).

The Order of British India, 1837–1947

Instituted in 1837 by the East India Company, this Order, worn around the neck, had two classes (First and Second) and was intended as a long-service award for native officers of the Company's Indian army. It continued in use after the removal of the Company's powers following the Indian Mutiny of 1857–59 and became obsolete in 1947. Some are known to have been awarded for specific acts of gallantry on campaign.

Awards announced in the *Gazette of India* and in the *London Gazette*.

The Order of Burma, 1940–47

This rare single-class Order was instituted by George VI as late as 1940, shortly after Burma had been separated from the Indian Empire for administrative purposes. It rewarded native officers of the Burma army and related forces in the same way as the *Order of British India* (q.v.) for the Indian army. After 1943, the Order was conferred as a form of distinguished service or gallantry award as much as for long service. Awards announced in the *Gazette of Burma* and in the *London Gazette*.

The Albert Medal, 1866–1971

Instituted in 1866, the *Albert Medal* was the first official medal to recognise bravery in saving life on a general scale. Though regarded as 'the civilian VC', it could also be awarded to military personnel for acts of gallantry not 'before the enemy' (e.g. dealing with fires in ammunition stores). (See photograph on p. 142.)

- *For Heroic Endeavour*, D V Henderson (Polstead, Hayward, 1988)
- *Heroes of the Albert Medal*, A Stanistreet (Honiton, Token, 2002).

The Distinguished Conduct Medal, 1854–1993

This venerable and highly regarded medal was for many years second only to the *Victoria Cross* as a gallantry award for the Other Ranks of the British Army. Instituted by Royal Warrant of 4 December 1854, it was effectively the first official British gallantry award, born out of the acts of bravery 'in the field' during the Crimean War (1854–56). It became obsolete in 1993 on the institution of the *Conspicuous Gallantry Cross* and the general abolition of medals (as opposed to Crosses) for gallantry. (See photograph on p. 131.)

Note: DCMs of specific type (along with MSMs and LSGC medals) were produced between 1895–1910 for some of the colonies (e.g. Canada and Natal), bearing their name on the obverse. Equally distinct types were produced from *c.* 1902–42 for the West African Frontier Force (WAFF) and King's African Rifles (KAR), bearing their titles on the obverse and with their own ribbon versions.

Award details:

- WO.391 (1854 to 1998)
- *The Distinguished Conduct Medal, 1855–1909*, 2nd edn, P E Abbott, (London, Hayward, 1987)
- *Recipients of the Distinguished Conduct Medal, 1914–20*, R W Walker (Birmingham, Midland Medals, 1981)
- *For Distinguished Conduct in the Field: The Register of the DCM, 1939–92*, G A Brown (n.p., Western Canadian Distributors, 1993)
- *The Register of the Distinguished Conduct Medal, 1920–92*, P McDermott (Polstead, Hayward, 1994)
- *The DCM to the British Commonwealth of Nations, 1920–1992*, G A Mackinley (Westmead, NSW, 1994)
- *The African DCM*, J Arnold (London, 2004).

The Conspicuous Gallantry Medal, 1855–1993

The CGM was essentially the Royal Navy and Royal Marines' counterpart of the DCM (q.v.), awarded 'to men who might at any time distinguish themselves by acts of conspicuous gallantry in action with the enemy'. Like the DCM, it was born out of the conditions of the Crimean War (1854–56) but only ten were awarded under the original Order in Council of 13 September 1855. The medal lapsed until 1874 when it was re-instituted at the conclusion of the Ashanti War. It became obsolete in 1993. (See photograph on p. 131.)

Award details:

- in ADM.1781-75 (index) and in ADM.171-61 (roll)

Above: The standard reverse of the *Distinguished Conduct Medal* (DCM) used on all awards from 1854–1993.

- *For Conspicuous Gallantry*, P McDermott (n.p., n.d.)
- *The Conspicuous Gallantry Medal*, G Brown and R Penhall (Vancouver, Pacific Publication Co., 1977).

The George Medal, 1940–to date

Instituted at the same time as the *George Cross* (q.v.) but for a lower level of gallantry, the GM is essentially an award for civilian 'acts of great bravery' and ranks next below the *George Cross*. Awards have been made to military personnel for actions not under enemy fire (e.g. bomb disposal, rescue attempts etc.) or where purely military awards were not appropriate and to foreign recipients. Approximately 2,000 medals and 25 bars have been conferred, about half of which were awarded to military recipients.

- *Dragons can be Defeated*, D V Henderson (London, Spink, 1984)
- *The George Medal*, W H Fevyer (London, Spink, 1980)
- *Fashioned into a Bow*, D V Henderson (Durham, 1995): George Medal to female recipients.

The Conspicuous Gallantry Medal (Flying), 1942–93

This rare silver medal was intended as the Air Forces' equivalent of the DCM to the Army or the existing CGM to the Royal Navy and Marines. Instituted by Royal Warrant of 10 November 1942, it was conferred for 'conspicuous gallantry in action against the enemy'. Apart from its ribbon, the award was identical in all respects to the existing CGM. Fewer than 100 were ever awarded. It became obsolete in 1993.

- *In Action with the Enemy: Holders of the CGM (Flying)*, A W Cooper (n.p., Kimber, 1986).

The King's Police Medal, 1909–54

Instituted by Royal Warrant of 7 July 1909, the KPM rewarded police and fire-service personnel in Britain and dominions for gallant or distinguished service. Prior to 1933, there was no distinction between those awarded for gallantry and those for distinguished service, but in that year two reverse types were introduced, with 'For Gallantry' or 'For Distinguished Service' in the reverse exergue. Bars were authorised for additional service.

In 1940, to recognise the exertions of the fire-fighting services during the Blitz and other air attacks, the medal was officially re-designated as the *King's Police and Fire Brigade Medal*, though the design remained the same. In 1950, it was decreed that the 'gallantry' version could only be awarded posthumously and in 1954 the award was discontinued, with separate medals being instituted for the police and fire services (see below).

- *Police Gallantry: the King's Police Medal, the King's Police and Fire Service Medal and the Queen's Police Medal 1909–79*, J P Farmery (n.p., 1996).

The Queen's Police Medal, 1954–to date

Instituted by Royal Warrant of 19 May 1954, the medal replaced the above award for police service. The reverse design retains that of the earlier KPM and also has two reverses, with 'For Distinguished Police Service' or 'For Gallantry' inscribed around the circumference.

The posthumous award for gallantry effectively became redundant in 1977 when the *George Medal* was made available to the police.

The Queen's Fire Service Medal, 1954–to date

Instituted by Royal Warrant of 19 May 1954, the medal replaced the above award for fire service. The reverse design retains that of the earlier KPM and also has two reverses, with 'For Distinguished Fire Service' or 'For Gallantry' inscribed around the circumference. The posthumous award for gallantry effectively became redundant in 1977 when the *George Medal* was made available to the fire services.

- *Police Gallantry: the King's Police Medal, the King's Police and Fire Service Medal and the Queen's Police Medal 1909–79*, J P Farmery (n.p., 1996).

The Edward Medal, 1907–71

This medal was introduced in 1907 to recognise civilian acts of gallantry at a level lower than that considered necessary to earn the *Albert Medal*. As first instituted, it was to reward bravery in saving life in mines and quarries, but in 1909 was extended to similar service in any industrial context. The two medals (mines and industry) bore different reverses. It became obsolete in 1971.

An example of the *Indian Distinguished Service Medal* (IDSM) which was issued between 1907–47. This type shows the rare 'crowned head' of George V. Used only between c. 1930–36, any gallantry award (IDSM, DCM, DFM, MM etc.) with this obverse is very rare as few were awarded.

- *For Heroic Endeavour*, D V Henderson (Polstead, Hayward, 1988).

The Indian Distinguished Service Medal, 1907–47

From 1837 onwards, the only gallantry medal available to Indian soldiers was the *Indian Order of Merit* (q.v.); they could not receive the DCM and the VC was not made available until 1911. The IDSM was instituted by Royal Warrant on 25 June 1907 to reward gallantry that did not reach the standard required for the IOM. Since fewer than 5,300 (including bars) were awarded prior to Indian independence in 1947, when it became obsolete, the medal is scarce. This is especially true of those bearing the Edward VII obverse and the George V 'crowned head' obverse of *c.* 1933–36.

Awards were announced in the *Gazette of India* and in the *London Gazette*.

- *The Indian Distinguished Service Medal*, Rana Chhina (Delhi, 2001).

The Burma Gallantry Medal, 1940–47

This rare award was instituted in 1940 at the same time as the *Order of Burma* (q.v.) It was intended to be the equivalent of the IDSM for the Burma army and associated local forces following Burma's separation from the Indian Empire. By the time the award became obsolete in 1947, when Burma became independent, only about 200 medals and 3 bars had been conferred.

Awards were announced in the *Gazette of Burma* and in the *London Gazette*.

The Distinguished Service Medal, 1914–93

The DSM was a lower tier award for naval forces introduced by Order in Council on 14 October 1914, at the outset of the First World War. Originally intended for the Other Ranks of the Royal Navy, ashore or afloat, in 1940 it was extended to men of the RAF serving with the Navy and in 1942 to Army personnel serving afloat (e.g. Royal Artillery gunners) and to men of the Merchant Navy.

Award details:

- ADM.171-75 (index)
- ADM.171-61 (details)

Above: The reverse of the *Distinguished Service Medal* (DSM). Many British medals have simple wording like this one on the reverse, in place of a more elaborate design.

The *Distinguished Flying Medal*, George VI obverse (left), with associated campaign awards for the Second World War. Some 6,500 DFMs were awarded for service in the Second World War.

- *The Distinguished Service Medal 1914–20*, W H Fevyer (Polstead, Hayward, 1982)
- *The Distinguished Service Medal 1939–46*, W H Fevyer (Polstead, Hayward, 1981).

The Military Medal, 1916–93

The MM was an award born out of the close-combat conditions of the First World War and the need to recognise the 'individual or associated acts of bravery' that were common occurrences but fell below the standard required for the DCM. It is in many respects the Army version of the DSM (q.v.) established in 1914. Instituted by Royal Warrant of 25 March 1916 (*London Gazette*, 5 April 1916), it could be awarded to the Other Ranks of the Army, Colonial Forces and (from 1944) to the Indian army. Women were declared eligible in June 1916 (the first being conferred for service in France in 1916 and during the Easter rebellion in Dublin in 1916) and foreign nationals could also receive the award. Some were also granted to personnel of the Royal Navy and Air Forces.

- *For Bravery in the Field: Recipients of the Military Medal, 1919–91*, C Bate and M Smith (n.p., Bayonet, 1991).

The Distinguished Flying Medal, 1918–93

Established by Royal Warrant and *London Gazette* of 3 June 1918 at the same time as the DFC (q.v.), it was effectively the Other Ranks equivalent of it.

Awarded for 'an act or acts of valour, courage or devotion to duty performed while flying in active operations against the enemy', it could also be awarded to Colonial and Dominion personnel.

- *The Distinguished Flying Medal: A Record of Courage, 1918–1982*, Ian Tavender (Polstead, Hayward, 1990)
- *The DFM Registers for the Second World War*, Ian Tavender (London, Savannah, 1999).

The Air Force Medal, 1918–93

The Other Ranks' equivalent of the AFC (q.v.), the AFM was instituted by Royal Warrant and *London Gazette* of 3 June 1918. It was essentially awarded 'for an act or acts of valour, courage or devotion to duty performed whilst flying though not in active operations against the enemy'. It was also conferred on Colonial and Dominion personnel but was rendered obsolete in 1993 when the AFC was made available to all ranks.

The Constabulary Medal, Ireland, 1842–1922

This rare silver medal was instituted in 1842 for the Irish Constabulary to reward gallantry and meritorious service. After 1872, it was awarded only for gallantry. The first award of the medal was not made until 1848 and the last in 1922, the year that the Royal Irish Constabulary was disbanded following the partition of Ireland.

The Indian Police Medal, 1932–50

Instituted in February 1932, this bronze medal rewarded European and Indian personnel of the Indian Police and Fire Brigades for gallantry or valuable service. Both services were eligible for the British KPM but as these were restricted to fifty per annum, it was felt that another award was required. The IPM was restricted to 200 awards in any single year.

The Burma Police Medal, 1937–48

Instituted in December 1937, this was another response to the separation of Burma from the Indian Empire for administrative reasons (see *Order of Burma*). The bronze medal was open to all ranks, European and Burmese, of the Burma police forces, frontier forces and fire brigades for gallantry or meritorious service, but with only twenty-five awards being made per year. This is a rare award, with approximately 141 issued: of which about 53 were awarded for gallantry, 80 for meritorious service and 8 unclassified.

The Colonial Police/Fire Brigade Medal, 1938

The *Colonial Police Medal* or *Fire Brigade Medal* was instituted in May 1938 to reward gallantry or meritorious service by members of colonial police forces and fire brigades. Only 150 were to be awarded in any year. In total, about 450 medals and 9 second award bars were conferred for gallantry and approximately 3,000 for meritorious service.

The Ceylon Police Medal, 1950–72

This silver medal, instituted in June 1950, replaced the *Colonial Police Medal* (above) as an award to the police services of Ceylon. It was abolished in 1972. There were two different reverse types, with inscription either 'For Gallantry' or 'For Merit'.

The Queen's Gallantry Medal, 1974–to date

This medal was instituted in June 1974 to recognise acts of gallantry by the emergency services and civilians, though forces' personnel can receive the award for gallantry in circumstances where military awards are not appropriate. Citizens of both Britain and the Commonwealth are eligible. (See photograph on p. 146.)

The Sea Gallantry Medal, 1855

The medal originated with the Merchant Shipping Act of 1854 which made provision for rewards for bravery in saving life at sea; it is the only award for gallantry instituted by Act of Parliament. The original award was a large 'table medal' of 58mm diameter, not intended for wear. Provision was made for gold, silver and bronze medals, but no gold medal is known. In 1904, the award was brought into line with other British gallantry medals by being reduced to a smaller, wearable medal of 33mm. (See photograph on p. 141.)

Examples of Unofficial and Society Awards for Civilian Gallantry

For a good overview of military and civilian awards prior to 1940, with many citations and details, see *Gallantry*, Sir A Wilson and J H F McEwen (London, 1939; reprinted Oxford, OUP, 1980). See also TNA guide 'Medals: Civilian Gallantry'.

The Royal Humane Society, 1774–to date

The first national society to make medallic awards for gallantry in saving life (mainly in silver and bronze) was the Royal Humane Society. Its medals and certificates are still awarded. (See photograph on p. 140.)

- *Acts of Gallantry*, Vol. II, W H Fevyer (London, 1999): roll of RHS medal recipients.

The Royal National Lifeboat Institution Medals, 1825–to date

The earliest national system for saving life at sea or in shipwrecks was established on 4 March 1824 with the establishment of the Royal National Institution for the Preservation of Life from Shipwreck (known as the Royal National Lifeboat Institution from 1854). It awarded medals in gold and silver from 1825 and from 1917 in bronze. Its medals are still awarded.

- *Lifeboat Gallantry: RNLI Medals and how they were won*, Barry Cox (London, Spink, 1998).

The Liverpool Shipwreck and Humane Society

This local society was one of many formed throughout the UK in the nineteenth century to reward gallantry in saving life in a variety of circumstances. Established in 1839, the Society subsequently awarded medals for saving life at sea, for saving life on land and for saving life from fire. Principal types:

The Liverpool Shipwreck and Humane Society's Marine Medals, 1844 (see photograph on p. 139)
The Liverpool Shipwreck and Humane Society's Fire Medal, 1882
The Liverpool Shipwreck and Humane Society's General Medal, 1894.

The Shipwrecked Fishermen and Mariners Royal Benevolent Society Medals, 1851

Founded in 1839 to provide aid to shipwrecked mariners and to the dependants of those lost at sea. It issued gold and silver medals from 1851 for 'heroic or praiseworthy exertions to save life from shipwreck etc.'.

The 'CQD' Medal, 1909

'CQD' was a wireless distress signal (commonly expanded as 'Come Quickly, Danger') and was the forerunner of the more familiar 'SOS'. The medal was instituted in 1909 following the collision between the White Star liner *Republic* and the Italian ship *Florida*. Following a CQD signal from the *Republic*, the liner *Baltic* came to the aid of the stricken ships and took aboard their passengers. The silver medal was awarded to the officers and crews of

One of the many types of medal produced by the insurers Lloyd's of London for gallant or distinguished service. This one is the rare award for bravery in saving life at sea, only awarded between 1940 and 1947.

all three ships by the passengers of the *Baltic* and *Republic* as a reward for their exertions in saving over 1,700 lives. Well-made copies exist.

The Life Saving Medal of the Order of St John, 1874

This medal was instituted by the Order in December 1874 to reward gallantry in saving life. First awarded in silver and bronze, a gold version was introduced in 1907.

Medals of the (Royal) Society for the Protection of Life from Fire, 1836

The Society, founded in 1836, awarded medals, certificates, watches and money to those who had saved life from fire. Several types of medal were awarded.

Lloyd's Medal for Saving Life at Sea, 1836

Lloyd's, the marine insurance company, introduced medals for life saving at sea in 1836. The first medal, 73mm in diameter, issued in silver or bronze, was not intended for wear and carried no suspension or ribbon. In 1896 the medal was reduced to a more standardised 36mm diameter and fitted with a ring suspension. It hung from a dark-blue ribbon with a central red band that was flanked by white stripes.

- *Lloyd's Medals, 1836–1998*, J Gawler (Toronto, 1998).

Lloyd's War Medal for Bravery at Sea, 1940

The Committee of Lloyd's introduced a silver medal in December 1940 to reward officers and men of the merchant and fishing fleets for exceptional bravery in time of war.

- *Lloyd's War Medal for Bravery at Sea*, G A Brown (Langley BC, Western Canadian Distributors Ltd, 1992)
- *Lloyd's Medals, 1836–1998*, J Gawler (Toronto, 1998).

The RMS *Carpathia* Medal for the *Titanic* Disaster, 1912

This was awarded to the crew of the *Carpathia* for perhaps the most-famous shipwreck of all time. On the night of 14 April 1912, the White Star liner *Titanic* struck an iceberg and sank during her maiden voyage. Of over 1,600 people aboard, only 711 were saved and taken aboard *Carpathia*. In gratitude for their efforts, the survivors paid for a medal to be given to the officers and crew, awarded in gold, silver or bronze according to rank. They are rare and highly collected but good fakes also exist.

The *Tayleur* Fund Medal, 1854–1913

A fund was established to benefit survivors of the ship *Tayleur*, which sank in Bantry Bay in January 1854. Surplus money from the fund was used to finance the award of this life-saving medal, which was available until December 1913 when the fund was transferred to the RNLI and separate medals ceased to be issued. However, it is believed that awards were made only between 1861 and 1875.

Chapter Fourteen

AWARDS FOR LONG AND MERITORIOUS SERVICE

For many years, collecting medals for long service and good conduct has been rather on the fringes of the hobby, perhaps suffering from a lack of glamour compared to medals for gallantry or campaign service. However, a long-service medal may have been the only award a man received and in many cases may reflect an interesting, active and varied career spanning many years and many tours of overseas' service.

The idea of rewarding service of long standing and which incorporated an element of good conduct came to the fore rather earlier than the general concept of awarding campaign and gallantry medals. The authorities were eager to retain experienced soldiers and sailors and to make it clear that long service and good conduct would be rewarded. This was especially so in the Navy where prior to 1853 men did not have to serve for continuous set periods but could move from ship to shore and back with potentially long gaps in their careers. In all branches of service, the loss of experienced men was keenly felt. Financial rewards (gratuities) of various amounts could be offered to those chosen as recipients of the long-service medal (who were very carefully selected), though they could equally be conferred without gratuity.

The earliest attempt to redress the issue came with the first *Army Long Service and Good Conduct Medal*, instituted in 1830. Unusually, the medal bore on its obverse not the effigy and titles of the monarch but a splendid 'trophy of

Above right: An example of an early regimentally produced long-service medal, in this case the ten-year award for the Queen's Royal (later West Surrey) Regiment. Many regiments issued such awards, in the early nineteenth century; some (like this one) very well produced. Others never did.

Left: The *Regular Army Long Service and Good Conduct Medal* (Elizabeth II obverse). This type, with flat suspension bar *Regular Army* was introduced in 1930 and is still awarded.

arms' designed by the noted engraver Benedetto Pistrucci. Over the years, numerous changes have been made to the suspension but the medal remains in use today. The original issue, from 1830–37, carried the Hanoverian arms in the centre of the royal escutcheon but when Britain relinquished control of Hanover in 1837 on the accession of Queen Victoria this element was removed. The 'trophy of arms' obverse remained in use until the reign of Edward VII (1901–10) when the usual effigy of the reigning monarch became the norm. It was also used on the *Distinguished Conduct Medal* prior to 1901.

Equally, the first *navy Long Service and Good Conduct Medal* of 1831 bore a decorative design – the reverse with simple wording and the recipient's engraved details and the obverse with a 'fouled anchor' and crown. This remained in use until 1848 when the design was completely changed. From that date to this, the naval LSGC has carried the reigning monarch's effigy and titles on the obverse and on the reverse a fine depiction of a wooden 'man of war'.

Allied to these medals for long service, awards and gratuities for especially meritorious service were also developed. The first was the *Army Meritorious Service Medal* (MSM), introduced in 1845. They were essentially rewards for exceptionally long service of a notably meritorious character and were always sparingly awarded, generally to senior NCOs. It is known, however, that some were conferred for good service on campaign (rather than for a longer period) but not until 1916 was this aspect properly addressed. In that year, prompted by the requirements of the First World War, 'immediate' awards were introduced, allowing the MSM to be granted for current war service. In 1917, awards for gallantry were instituted, though this was generally not for gallantry 'before the enemy' and the medal carried no indication of the fact. Awards of both the 'immediate' and 'gallantry' MSMs ceased in 1928.

Above: The first *Navy Long Service and Good Conduct Medal*, known as the 'Anchor' type. The reverse is beautifully engraved with the recipient's details. Awarded 1830–47, when replaced by the larger type shown on p.172.

Right: The reverse of the *Army Meritorious Service Medal*, which has remained the same since its inauguration in 1845. The ribbon was originally the same as that for the *Army Long Service and Good Conduct Medal* (plain dark red) but was altered to avoid confusion in 1917.

Like the basic long-service awards, the Army MSM was followed by a range of similar MSMs for the other services, eventually including colonial and Indian versions. The difference between the simple long-service awards and those for 'meritorious service' was length of time – the MSMs generally required much longer service – and an irreproachable character or distinctly distinguished service. Thereafter, long-service and good-conduct medals were created in a bewildering variety, covering the plethora of part-time military and naval units formed over the course of years in Britain and throughout the Empire. The same was true for awards to police and fire service and colonial military and police units. There is no space in the present work to outline all of these awards, but the following is a simple indication of the sheer range and variety of medals for long service and good conduct.

Meritorious Service Awards: British and Imperial

The Army Meritorious Service Medal, 1845–to date

Introduced in 1845 to reward specially long and/or meritorious service by NCOs, since 1956 the recipient must have served a minimum of twenty-seven years to qualify and it is only selectively granted – length of service is not the only qualification. It was briefly granted as an 'immediate' award for specially meritorious war service between 1916 and 1928, a circumstance originally generated by the need to reward forces' personnel for good work not generally 'before the enemy' during the war. These 'immediate' awards ceased in 1928 (the *British Empire Medal* often serving as an appropriate reward thereafter) and the MSM once again became a long and meritorious service award for NCOs.

Registers of awards from 1846 to 1919 are in WO.101.

- *The Annuity Meritorious Service Medal*, Ian McInnes (n.p., Jade, 1994)
- *The Meritorious Service Medal: Immediate Awards 1916–128*, Ian McInnes (n.p., Jade, 1992)
- *For Gallantry in the Performance of Military Duty*, Maj. J D Sainsbury (London, Samson Books, 1980).

The Royal Marines Meritorious Service Medal, 1849–1951; 1977–to date

Always a rare medal, it was awarded to serving sergeants of irreproachable and meritorious character, with at least twenty-four years' service, of which fourteen had to be in the rank of sergeant. Re-established in 1977.

The RAF Meritorious Service Medal, 1918–28; 1977–to date

Available, without annuity, to men and women of the rank of sergeant or above who have served for a minimum of twenty-seven years, who already possess the LSGC medal and who have maintained irreproachable conduct and a high standard of service. The award, which was re-established in 1977, is not automatic.

- *The Meritorious Service Medal to Aerial Forces*, Ian McInnes (Chippenham Picton, 1984).

The Royal Naval Meritorious Service Medal, 1919–28; 1977–to date

Re-instituted on 1 December 1977 after only a brief initial life-span of 1919–28, the silver medal is available (without annuity) to personnel of the RN, RM, QARNS and WRNS. Recipients must be senior serving NCOs, the main qualification being twenty-seven years' service and possession of the LSGC and three Good Service badges. There is no automatic entitlement to the medal.

- *The Meritorious Service Medal to Naval Forces*, Ian McInnes (n.p., 1983).

The Indian Army Meritorious Service Medal: for Europeans, 1848–73

Introduced by the government of India in May 1848. It was awarded to the European personnel of the forces of the East India Company and conferred upon sergeants, serving or already discharged, for distinguished or meritorious service. An annuity of not more than £20 accompanied the award.

The Indian Army Meritorious Service Medal, 1888–1947

A distinctive MSM purely for the Indian personnel of the Indian army was only instituted in 1888 and was awarded with annuity to senior NCOs. The minimum service requirement was eighteen years of distinctly meritorious service but it was very sparingly conferred. It became obsolete in 1947.

Army Long-service Awards: Regular Army, Militia, Volunteers and Territorials

The Army Long Service and Good Conduct Medal, 1830–to date

The first official medal for long service and good conduct – and both elements were important – was instituted in 1830 by King William IV. Originally awarded for twenty-one years' service in the infantry or twenty-four in the cavalry, the time requirement was reduced and standardised to eighteen years in 1870. It has gone through several changes in design and is still awarded.

Registers of awards from 1831 to 1975 are in WO.102.

- *The Army Long Service and Good Conduct Medal 1830–1848*, I McInnes and B Gregson (n.p., Jade, 1996 with later supplements).

Top right: The *Indian Army Meritorious Service Medal*, with 'veiled head' of Queen Victoria. The design – featuring a band of lotus leaves and flowers – is the same for the contemporary *Indian Army Long Service and Good Conduct Medal*, except for altered wording. Both were only awarded to Indian soldiers.

Left: An example of an *Army Long Service and Good Conduct Medal*, as awarded to commonwealth forces. Many different types of local suspension bar were issued, this one bearing the title of the colony of Basutoland.

The Volunteer Officer's Decoration (VD), 1892–1908

This attractive open-work decoration – a novel design for its time – was instituted in July 1892 to reward officers of the Volunteer forces (established 1859–60) for twenty years' service as a commissioned officer. Time spent in the ranks counted half towards the award.

- *The Volunteer Officer's Decoration*, J M A Tamplin (London, Spink, 1980).

The Territorial Decoration (TD), 1908–30

The *Territorial Decoration* was instituted in August 1908, following the establishment of the Territorial Force and replaced the *Volunteer Officer's Decoration*. In design, it was exactly the same as its predecessor, with the crowned cypher of the reigning monarch in gilt in the centre. Qualification was twenty years' service as a commissioned officer in the Territorial Force; service in the ranks counted half towards the qualification, while war service counted double. It was replaced in 1930 by the *Efficiency Decoration*.

- *The Territorial Decoration 1908–30*, J M A Tamplin (London, Spink, 1983).

The Efficiency Decoration (ED), 1930–99

A new long-service decoration was introduced in September 1930 to replace the old *Territorial Decoration*, the *Indian Volunteer Decoration* and the *Colonial Auxiliary Decoration* (q.v). The initial qualification was twenty years' service, but in 1949 this was changed to twelve years' continuous commissioned service in Britain, though twenty years continued to be required within the Commonwealth. Previous service in the ranks counted half towards the award, while war service counted double.

- *The Efficiency Decoration 1930*, J M A Tamplin (London, Spink, 1987).

Top right: The *Volunteer Officers' Decoration* (VD). An unusual open-work design to reward officers in the Volunteer Forces for long service. The reverse was plain but is usually found engraved to its recipient.

Left: The *Efficiency Decoration*, with ribbon and top bar *Territorial* as introduced in 1982. Awarded to officers in the Territorial Army for twelve years' service, it was one of the awards replaced by the *Volunteer Reserve Services Medal* in 2000.

The Army Emergency Reserve Decoration (ED), 1952–67

Instituted in November 1952, the Decoration was awarded for twelve years' commissioned service in the Army Emergency Reserve. Officers commissioned into this Reserve or into the Army Supplementary Reserve between 8 August 1924 and 15 May 1948 who transferred into the Regular Army Reserve of Officers after ten years' service were eligible. War service counted double and service in the ranks counted half.

- *The Army Emergency Reserve Decoration and Efficiency Medal (Army Emergency Reserve)*, J M A Tamplin (London, Spink, 1998).

The Volunteer Long Service and Good Conduct Medal, 1894–1908/30

Instituted in May 1894, this medal rewarded service of at least twenty years in the ranks of the Volunteer forces which had been established throughout the country after 1859. It was superseded by the *Territorial Force Long Service and Good Conduct Medal* in Britain in 1908 but remained in use in India until 1930.

- *The Volunteer Long Service Medal*, J M A Tamplin (London, Spink, 1980).

The Territorial Force Efficiency Medal, 1908–21

The Other Ranks award for long service and good conduct in the new Territorial Force was established in June 1908 and replaced the earlier *Volunteer Long Service and Good Conduct Medal* in Britain. The silver medal (unusually an oval) was awarded to 'efficient' NCOs and Other Ranks of the Territorial Force who completed twelve years' service and twelve annual trainings.

- *The Territorial Force Efficiency Medal 1908–21 and the Territorial Efficiency Medal, 1922–30*, J M A Tamplin (London, Spink, 1980).

The Territorial Efficiency Medal, 1921–30

With the reorganisation of the Territorial Force after the First World War and the creation of the Territorial Army, a new long-service medal was instituted. It was identical to the TFEM of 1908–21 (above), except that the word 'Force' was removed from the reverse lettering and the ribbon was slightly altered. It was replaced by the *Efficiency Medal* in 1930.

- *The Territorial Force Efficiency Medal 1908–21 and the Territorial Efficiency Medal, 1922–30*, J M A Tamplin (London, Spink, 1980).

The Efficiency Medal, 1930–99

The *Efficiency Medal*, a new award for long and 'efficient' service in various part-time and volunteer forces, was introduced in October 1930. It replaced the *Territorial Efficiency Medal*, the *Militia Long Service and Good Conduct Medal* and the *Special Reserve Long Service and Good Conduct Medal* in Britain, along with the old *Volunteer Long Service and Good Conduct Medal* in India and the *Colonial Auxiliary Long Service and Good Conduct Medal* in the Colonies. A scroll bar suspension bore the subsidiary title of the award – 'Territorial' or 'Militia' as appropriate, or the name of an overseas territory (many types, e.g. 'Australia', 'India', 'Malaya', 'Basutoland' etc.). The basic qualification was twelve years' continuous and 'efficient' service. War service or service in West Africa counted double.

The Efficiency Medal (Army Emergency Reserve), 1953–76

This medal, instituted by Royal Warrant of 1 September 1956, was identical to the *Efficiency Medal* (q.v.), except that the suspension bar bore the wording 'Army Emergency Reserve'. It rewarded twelve years' service in the ranks of the Army Emergency Reserve or for service in the Supplementary Reserve between 1924 and 1948 prior to transfer to the Army Emergency Reserve.

The Imperial Yeomanry Long Service and Good Conduct Medal, 1904–8

The county Yeomanry force of part-time, volunteer cavalry was designated 'Imperial Yeomanry' in 1900 during the Boer War. This short-lived and quite rare oval silver medal was authorised in December 1904 for members of the Imperial Yeomanry who were serving on or after 9 November 1904 and who completed ten years' service and ten annual trainings and were of good character and conduct.

- *The Imperial Yeomanry Long Service and Good Conduct Medal,* J M A Tamplin (London, Spink, 1978).

Above: The *Territorial Efficiency Medal* (1930–99); obverse for Elizabeth II.

The Militia Long Service and Good Conduct Medal, 1904–30

Like the Imperial Yeomanry award (above), this short-lived and rare oval silver medal was authorised in December 1904. It rewarded members of the old county Militia force who were serving on or after 9 November 1904 and who completed eighteen years' service and fifteen trainings.

- *The Militia Long Service and Good Conduct Medal*, J M A Tamplin (London, Spink, 1979).

The Special Reserve Long Service and Good Conduct Medal, 1908–36

This rare medal was authorised in June 1908 to reward the NCOs and Other Ranks of the newly formed Special Reserve (formerly the Militia) who completed fifteen years' service and attended fifteen trainings. Service with the Militia, Imperial Yeomanry, Volunteers or Territorial Forces was counted towards the time qualification, provided that the last five years had been spent in the Special Reserve.

The Volunteer Reserves Service Medal, 1999–to date

In a move to standardise awards to volunteer forces of all kinds, this new medal was introduced in 1999. It retains the silver, oval format of the earlier TA and associated awards and is awarded for ten years' 'efficient service', with bars for further periods of five years. The medal replaced in one fell swoop the *RNR Decoration*, the *RNR Long Service and Good Conduct Medal*, the *Efficiency Decoration*, the *Efficiency Medal* and the *Air Efficiency Award*.

The Ulster Defence Regiment Long Service and Good Conduct Medal, 1982–2006

Introduced in 1982, this silver medal was essentially the standard *British Army Long Service and Good Conduct Medal*, post-1930, but with suspension bar reading 'U.D.R.'. It was awarded for fifteen years' service in the permanent staff of the UDR after 1 April 1970 and bars were awarded for further periods of fifteen years.

Above: The *Volunteer Reserve Services Medal* (VRSM), introduced in 1999. It replaced a number of existing long-service awards to part-time volunteer forces as part of an attempt to standardise the system.

The Ulster Defence Regiment Medal, 1982

Similar to the above medal, this award was also instituted in 1982 and was conferred on the part-time personnel, both officers and men, of the UDR for twelve years' continuous service after 1 April 1970.

The Cadet Forces' Medal, 1950–to date

The cupro-nickel medal introduced in February 1950 was awarded to commissioned officers and adult instructors for twelve years' service with the Cadets in Britain and in Commonwealth countries. A bar could be awarded for further periods of eight years' service.

- *Medal Roll of the Cadet Forces' Medal*, D F Collins (Ongar, 1989).

Naval Long-service Awards

The Royal Navy Long Service and Good Conduct Medal, 1831–to date

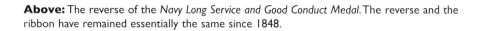

Instituted by William IV ('the Sailor King') in August 1831, it was to be awarded to petty officers, sailors and marines of twenty-one years' service and irreproachable character. The period required was briefly reduced to ten years in 1874 but shortly afterwards was increased to fifteen years. In exceptional circumstances, the medal could be awarded without the strict application of the length of service requirement. It is still awarded, with the reverse design of a sailing warship unaltered since 1848.

- *Naval Long Service and Good Conduct Medals 1830–1990*, K J Douglas-Morris (London, 1991).

The Royal Naval Reserve Decoration (RD), 1908–99

This decoration was awarded for fifteen years' service as a commissioned officer in the Royal Naval Reserve. Service as midshipman did not count, but wartime service counted double towards the service requirement.

Above: The reverse of the *Navy Long Service and Good Conduct Medal*. The reverse and the ribbon have remained essentially the same since 1848.

The '1915 Trio' with *Royal Naval Reserve Decoration* (RD) at right. This attractive but simple open-work award bears the cypher of the reigning monarch in the centre. The *Victory Medal* (third from left) carries the *Mentioned in Dispatches* oak-leaf spray of 1914–20.

The Royal Naval Volunteer Reserve Decoration, 1908–66

This decoration was similar in design to the *RNR Decoration* (q.v.). Instituted in 1908, it could be conferred on officers of the RNVR for twenty years' service, not necessarily continuous.

The Royal Naval Reserve Long Service and Good Conduct Medal, 1908–2000

This silver medal, with straight bar suspension, was instituted in September 1908 and awarded to men of the Royal Naval Reserve who had completed fifteen years' service with related periods of training. War service would count double towards the award.

The Royal Naval Volunteer Reserve Long Service and Good Conduct Medal, 1908–58

This silver medal was identical in design to the *RNR Long Service and Good Conduct Medal* (q.v.) – only the naming on the rim specified the service – and was awarded for twelve years' service with the appropriate number of training periods.

The Royal Fleet Reserve Long Service and Good Conduct Medal, 1919

This silver medal was essentially the same as those for the RNR and RNVR except that the ribbon was suspended from a simple ring, not a bar. It was awarded for fifteen years' service in the Fleet Reserve, with conduct assessed as 'Very Good'. Service in the RN counted, so long as the *RN Long Service and Good Conduct Medal* had not been awarded.

The Royal Naval Auxiliary Sick Berth Reserve Long Service and Good Conduct Medal, 1919–49

The Auxiliary Sick Berth Reserve was a volunteer medical corps drawn from the St John Ambulance Brigade to provide additional medical orderlies and attendants on ships in time of war. The qualification time was fifteen years' service, the first award being made in 1919. The Reserve was disbanded in 1949. The medal is exactly like the *RNR Long Service and Good Conduct Medal* – only the naming details on the rim indicate the branch.

The Royal Naval Wireless Auxiliary Reserve Long Service and Good Conduct Medal, 1939–57

This medal is similar in design to the *RNR* and *RNVR Long Service and Good Conduct* medals and only the initials 'RNWAR' in the recipient's naming details identify the unit. It was awarded for twelve years' service, with time in the RNVR allowed to count towards the requirement. Bars could be awarded for additional periods of twelve years.

The Royal Naval Auxiliary Services Long Service and Good Conduct Medal, 1965–94

Instituted in July 1965, this cupro-nickel medal was granted to both officers and Other Ranks for twelve years' satisfactory service in the Royal Naval Auxiliary Services (founded in 1962) or in its predecessor, the Royal Naval Minewatching Service, founded in 1952.

The Rocket Apparatus Volunteer Long Service and Good Conduct Medal, 1911–68

Instituted in 1911 by the Board of Trade, this medal was awarded for twenty years' service with the Rocket Life Saving Apparatus Volunteers – a long time requirement. The volunteers manned shore-based line-firing apparatus to reach grounded or stranded ships and help in the evacuation of crews and passengers.

The Coastguard Auxiliary Long Service Medal , 1968–to date

This award succeeded the previous *Rocket Apparatus Volunteer Long Service and Good Conduct Medal.*

The Royal Fleet Auxiliary Service Medal, 2001

Created in July 2001, the medal can be awarded to all ranks of the Royal Fleet Auxiliary (RFA), the service that repairs and re-supplies warships and troopships at sea. Most of its personnel are civilians, classed as Merchant Navy rather than Royal Navy, with naval officers and senior ratings performing specialist functions. The medal is granted for twenty years' service, with bars for further periods of ten years.

RAF Long-service Awards

The Royal Air Force Long Service and Good Conduct Medal, 1919–to date

Founded on 1 April 1918, the Royal Air Force amalgamated the old RFC and RNAS and was the last of the three major forces to institute its own Long Service and Good Conduct Medal. Created in July 1919, the medal rewarded non-commissioned ranks of the RAF who had served for eighteen years with irreproachable conduct. In 1977, the period of service was reduced to fifteen years. However, it could also be awarded before 1945 without the time requirement being fulfilled for distinguished service in time of war or emergency.

The Air Efficiency Award, 1942–99

This was the RAF equivalent of the Territorial Army's *Efficiency Medal* – for service in the part-time volunteer forces of the RAF. Instituted in September 1942, it was granted for ten years' long and 'efficient' service in the Auxiliary and Volunteer air forces of Britain and the Commonwealth. Bars could be awarded for further periods of ten years. It was superseded in 1999 by the new *Volunteer Reserves Service Medal* (q.v.).

Examples of Imperial and Colonial Long-service Awards

Many dominions and colonies had their own range of such awards, of which this is a selection.

The Long Service and Good Conduct Medal for Europeans in the Indian Army, 1848–73

Prior to the transfer of power from the East India Company in 1858 the EIC had employed European NCOs and Other Ranks in its Indian regiments, departments and corps. This silver medal was instituted in May 1848 and was awarded on discharge to European soldiers of the EIC forces who had rendered twenty-one years' meritorious service.

The Indian Army Long Service and Good Conduct Medal, 1884–1947

A separate long-service award for the Indian soldiers of the Indian army was long in coming. Previously, they could receive the standard British issue, though examples are rare. The new silver medal was instituted in 1888 to reward twenty years' service. The 'good conduct' element was strictly applied and the medal was sparingly awarded.

The Indian Volunteer Officers' Decoration (IVD), 1899–1930

A decoration for British Officers serving with the Indian Volunteer Forces was authorised in May 1899 but for some time they received the existing British *Volunteer Officers' Decoration* in a distinctive Indian version with the imperial cypher 'VRI' instead of 'VR' in the centre. Not until 1903 was a newly designed award introduced, this being an unusual open-work silver and gilt design. The basic qualification was eighteen years' service in the Indian Volunteers, with time in the ranks counting half. After 1930, the *Efficiency Decoration* (q.v.) with top bar *India* was awarded to officers of the Volunteers' successors, the Auxiliary Forces of India (AFI).

Above: Obverse of the *Long Service and Good Conduct Medal for Europeans in the Indian Army.* The 'trophy of arms' design has the East India Company arms in the centre.

- *The Colonial Auxiliary Forces Officers' Decoration and Indian Volunteer Officers' Decoration*, J M A Tamplin (London, Spink, 1981).

The Colonial Auxiliary Forces Officers' Decoration, 1899–1930

Instituted, like the *Indian Volunteer Decoration* (above) in May 1899, it was essentially the same as the Indian type, except that it bore the wording 'Colonial Auxiliary Forces'. The basic qualification was twenty years' service in the reserve forces (Volunteers or Militias) of the Dominions and Colonies, other than India. Service in the ranks counted half towards the time requirement.

- *Canadian Recipients of the Colonial Auxiliary Forces Officers' Decoration and Colonial Forces Long Service Medal*, S M Pallas (n.p., n.d.)
- *The Colonial Auxiliary Forces Officers' Decoration and Indian Volunteer Officers' Decoration*, J M A Tamplin (London, Spink, 1981).

The Colonial Auxiliary Forces Long Service Medal, 1899–1930

This silver medal, the Other Ranks' version of the *Colonial Auxiliary Forces Decoration* (above) was instituted by the same Royal Warrant in 1899 and, like the decoration, was awarded for twenty years' service in the colonial Volunteers or Militias, excluding India. Service in West Africa counted double, as did service in the First World War.

- *Canadian Recipients of the Colonial Auxiliary Forces Officers' Decoration and Colonial Forces Long Service Medal*, S M Pallas (n.p., n.d.)
- *The Colonial Auxiliary Forces Officers' Decoration and Indian Volunteer Officers' Decoration*, J M A Tamplin (London, Spink, 1981).

The Permanent Forces of the Empire Beyond the Seas Long Service and Good Conduct Medal, 1909–30

Instituted in 1909, this replaced various short-lived colonial long-service medals of 1895–1909 and was in turn superseded by the 1930 *Army Long Service and Good Conduct Medal* with the appropriate Colony or Dominion title on the suspender bar. The medal was awarded to NCOs and men of the Permanent Overseas Forces of the Empire (i.e. not part-time forces) for eighteen years' service with decidedly good conduct.

The Royal West African Frontier Force and King's African Rifles Long Service and Good Conduct Medal, 1903 and 1907

A separate long-service and good-conduct medal was authorised for both the West African Frontier Force (WAFF) in September 1903 and for the

King's African Rifles (KAR) in March 1907. They were granted for eighteen years' service with good conduct. They were not awarded after about 1942.

The South African Permanent Force Long Service and Good Conduct Medal, 1939–52

Instituted in December 1939, this medal was essentially the South African version of the standard British military long-service and good-conduct medal. It was awarded to the non-commissioned ranks of the South African Permanent (i.e. full-time) Forces for eighteen years' service.

Police and Fire-service Long-service Awards

The Police Long Service and Good Conduct Medal, 1951–to date

Instituted by Royal Warrant of 14 June 1951, this cupro-nickel medal is the standard police medal for long service and good conduct and is awarded to full-time police officers for twenty-two years' service.

The Special Constabulary Long Service and Good Conduct Medal, 1919

A bronze medal to reward long service in the volunteer and part-time Special Constabulary was introduced in August 1919 when the continuation of the war-raised force, which was deemed to have rendered excellent service, was confirmed. The medal is granted for nine years' unpaid service, with at least fifty duties per annum.

The Royal Ulster Constabulary Service Medal, 1982

This cupro-nickel medal was authorised in 1982 for members of the Royal Ulster Constabulary and its Reserve for eighteen months' continuous service since 1 January 1971. Now obsolete.

The Colonial Police Long Service Medal, 1934

Instituted in 1934, this silver medal rewarded junior officers and members of the various colonial police forces for eighteen years' full-time and exemplary service. Bars could be awarded for further periods of service.

The Royal Canadian Police Long Service Medal, 1933

Instituted in January 1933, this silver medal was granted to members of the Royal Canadian Mounted Police, the famous 'Mounties', for twenty years' service with good conduct. It was awarded retrospectively to those who had retired by 1933. Further service bars were awarded in bronze (for a total of twenty-five years' service) or in silver (thirty years) or in gold (thirty-five years). Only one bar may be worn.

The Fire Brigade Long Service Medal, 1954

Instituted 1 June 1954, this cupro-nickel medal is awarded to all ranks of the local-authority fire brigades, full or part-time, for twenty years' service with good conduct.

The Colonial Fire Brigade Long Service Medal, 1934

The Colonial Fire Brigade's equivalent of the *Colonial Police Long Service and Good Conduct Medal* was instituted in 1934 and awarded to junior officers and lower ranks for eighteen years' full-time service. Bars were awarded for further periods of service.

The Northern Ireland Prison Service Medal, 2002–to date

Instituted in February 2002, this medal is awarded to members of the Northern Ireland Prison Service for meritorious service. It was to be awarded to those who had spent at least five years in the service and could also be granted to those who have acted in support of the Northern Ireland Prison Service.

Other Examples of Long-service Awards

The Royal Household Faithful Service Medals, 1872–to date

Queen Victoria instituted the first medal for long and loyal service in the Royal Household in 1872. Usually service of twenty-five years was required and bars could be conferred for extra periods of ten years. The silver medal is still awarded.

The Royal Observer Corps Medal, 1950

The Royal Observer Corps traced its origins in the 'coast watchers' and, more formally, to the civil-defence-related organisations of the Second World War. After that they were part of Britain's air defence and early warning system. A medal was instituted in January 1950 and was awarded to officers and observers who completed twelve years' satisfactory service, with bars for further periods of twelve years. The force was stood down in 1991.

The Civil Defence Long Service Medal, 1961–68

The oval cupro-nickel medal was introduced in March 1961 for those who rendered fifteen years' service with a number of associated civil-defence and voluntary medical organisations (e.g. the Auxiliary Fire Service) and was extended in 1963 to Malta, Hong Kong and Gibraltar. Bars could be awarded for further periods of fifteen years. The Civil Defence Corps, under which most of these bodies were united, was disbanded in 1968.

The Women's (Royal) Voluntary Service Long Service Medal, 1961

The WVS was founded during the Second World War to aid civilians affected by the war. After the war, it concentrated on helping isolated people, particularly the elderly, or those in hospital. The Queen became patron of the WVS in 1956 and the service was granted the title 'Royal' in 1966. A long-service medal was inaugurated in 1961, fifteen years' service being required, with bars conferred for extra periods of twelve years.

The Voluntary Medical Service Medal, 1932

This medal was instituted to reward long service in voluntary medical associations, principally the British Red Cross Society and the St Andrew's Ambulance Corps in Scotland. It is awarded for fifteen years' service, with bars conferred for each additional five-year period. These have a central Geneva cross or saltire of St Andrew according to the organisation of the recipient. The medal was originally issued in silver, but from the 1960s onwards has been awarded in cupro-nickel.

The Service Medal of the Order of St John, 1898

The only current medal that still bears the head of Queen Victoria is the service medal awarded by the Order of the Hospital of St John of Jerusalem in England. Originally given for fifteen years' service in the Order in Britain, or twelve years' in the Dominions or ten in the Colonies, the requirement has been amended to twelve years' service in Britain and Commonwealth countries, excluding South Africa, New Zealand, Canada and Australia, where ten years' service is required. The award can also be granted without this time requirement for exceptionally distinguished service to the Order.

Appendix One

USING THE INTERNET

There is no doubt that the World Wide Web or Internet will grow immensely in significance as a research tool over time. Although it is true to say that the printed word – regimental, campaign, battle and personal histories in books, magazines and journals – will continue to be of great value, the Internet is clearly set to become the major recourse for researchers of all kinds. However, caution should be exercised when accessing information from some websites as there are often no guarantees regarding the accuracy of what is provided.

Using the Internet at its most basic level is straightforward; merely typing into a major search engine like Yahoo (www.uk.yahoo.com) or Google (www.google.co.uk) the name of a war, campaign, battle, warship, squadron or military unit will produce a range of possible sites. Some of the most general sources of information are online encyclopaedias, like Wikipedia (www.wikipedia.org), which has a good range of articles on all sorts of military history and related topics. Many of these general sites also offer links to other more specialist locations, societies and information.

The most important site for any serious researcher of military related family history must be TNA at Kew, where most of what remains of Britain's official records relating to the Army, Navy, Marines, air forces and others is located. Its website (www.nationalarchives.gov.uk), with its 'Access2Archives' and 'Documents Online' sections, should be the foundation for any study, whether it be for a major campaign or an individual. It has produced an excellent range of guides to what is available (see above, pp. 75, 123–24) which is regularly expanded as new records are released into the public domain, and which can be read online or downloaded.

Another major archive is the British Library (www.bl.uk), a copyright library holding a vast range of books as well as newspaper collections and archives on the Empire and the Commonwealth. Its African, Oriental and

Pacific collections (www.bl.uk/collections/asiapacificafrica.html) are important for the archives of the former India Office, and hold the remaining records of the East India Company and the Madras, Bombay, Bengal and unified Indian armies, including medal rolls, dispatches, Indian gazettes, army lists and actual service records for some Indian army officers. TNA and national war memorials of Scotland, Ireland, Canada, New Zealand, Australia and South Africa also have online sites and some (like the Australian war archives at www.naa.gov.au. and its memorials at www.awm.gov.au) offer access to casualty lists and even actual service records for various periods. Other major archives worth consulting are held by:

- The National Maritime Museum at Greenwich (www.nmm.ac.uk)
- The Royal Naval Museum at Portsmouth (www.royalnavalmuseum.org.)
- The Royal Marines Museum at Southsea (www.royalmarinesmuseum.co.uk)
- The RAF Museum at Hendon (www.rafmuseum.org.uk) and its outstations at Duxford and Cosford.

Also important are the larger corps museums such as:

- Firepower, the museum of the Royal Artillery (www.firepower. org.uk.)
- The Royal Engineers Museum at Gillingham (www.royalengineers.org.uk).

Bear in mind that museums can offer a wide range of information – like specialist books, photographic collections, unit journals, official handbooks and publications, original documents and (in some cases) personal records, etc. – though fees may be charged for their research services.

For those seeking casualty information and grave locations, the Commonwealth War Graves Commission is the starting point. Responsible for the graves and memorials of the war dead of Britain and the Commonwealth after 1914, its online database at www.cwgc.org is an essential reference, naming individuals, date of death, location of grave or memorial and sometimes biographical or family details, if these had been provided by next of kin at the time. Other good sites in this field are the 'UK National Inventory of War Memorials' (available via the Imperial War Museum site at www.iwm.org.uk) and the 'British War Memorial Project' (www.britishwargraves.org.uk). The official War Office Casualty Lists for

1914–18 and 1939–45 (which offer slightly different detail than those of the CWGC) are not yet fully accessible online, but are commercially available in printed form for all services in the First World War and on CD for Army casualties (only) of the First World War and the Second World War. It should also be borne in mind that local libraries, county record offices and regional newspapers might also contain useful information on local people, regiments and units, including casualty and battle reports, obituaries and honours to local men and women for war service. See the 'Access2Archives' pages (at www.a2a.org.uk) at TNA for links to regional sites.

The main general museum on the history of Britain's Army since 1660 is the National Army Museum, Royal Hospital Road, Chelsea (www.national-army-museum.ac.uk), which apart from its extensive collections and displays, has a large library and archive that is available for use by researchers. For background information on regimental history, some general sites are excellent in providing a basis for research on a particular unit. It is beyond the scope of the present work to list all the regimental museum site details but the following are good starting points. The current British Army website (www.army.uk) has a useful museums' section, which has outline information on the major regimental and other military museums in Britain. Equally important in this respect is the Army Museums' Ogilby Trust (AMOT), the website (www.armymuseums.org.uk) of which offers information, links and contact details on British military and regimental museums. It also publishes the standard guide to regimental and military museums in Britain. For details not only of British but also Imperial and Commonwealth regiments and units, www.regiments.org is a useful site. From locations such as these, it is possible to visit the site of a relevant local museum, read about their regiment's history online or contact the museum itself for further information.

Most major campaigns and even single battles are covered by their own dedicated websites, the work of professional historians or institutions or of dedicated amateurs and interested collectors. Using search engines, it is a simple matter to locate these sites. An excellent general site is that of the Victorian Military Society (www.vms.org.uk) and other good examples are the Crimean War Research Society (www.crimeanwar.org), the Anglo-Zulu War Society (www.anglozuluwar.com) and the Boer War site (www.angloboerwar.com). On the Indian army of 1901–39, a good site is For the King-Emperor (www.king-emperor.com) and there are sites on Scottish, Irish, South African, New Zealand and Canadian forces, to name a few. A good site on warships in general is www.pbenyon.plus.com/Naval.html, as is the 'William Loney' site (on the mid-nineteenth century: www.home.wxs.nl/~pdavis). For the rest, searching for any squadron, ship or unit by name will often produce detailed information, including specific old comrades and reunion sites as well as purely historical detail. Many of the larger sites, whether they have local or national interests, offer online discussion groups, regular e-mailing lists and printed journals.

Not surprisingly, especially given the interest in genealogical research that has been apparent recently, the major wars of the twentieth century are well covered, both in a general sense and from the point of view of individual campaigns and battles or regimental service. On the First World War, the Imperial War Museum in Lambeth, London (www.iwm.org.uk) is of major importance, with extensive archives and photographic collections. Other good general sites are the 'Regimental Warpath, 1914–18' (www.warpath.orbat.com) which covers (or will eventually cover) all British and Commonwealth forces involved in the war. Other developing sites that offer a wealth of information are 'The British Army in the Great War' (at www.1914-18.net) and 'World War One Trenches on the Net '(www.worldwar1.com), which covers a wide range of 1914–18 related subject matter, as does www.firstworldwar.com. 'The Long Long Trail' at www.1914-1918.net/grandad/grandad.htm is also a useful site; it has, for example, an alphabetical listing of British prisoners of war whose interviews and reports survive and are held in TNA under WO.161. Other good sites – among many – are www.greatwar.co.uk and www.ww1 battlefields.co.uk.

Useful organisations (which also produce regular specialist journals) are the Western Front Association (www.westernfront.co.uk and www.westernfrontassociation.com) and the Great War Society (the British branch of which is at www.thegreatwarsociety.com.). Specific campaigns within the First World War are also increasingly being reflected on the Internet. Examples are www.ypressalient.co.uk (on Ypres), 'The Passchendaele Archives' (www.passchendale.be), a Belgian site dedicated to the memory of all those who served and died in the third battle of Ypres, 'Somme Battlefields' (at www.somme-battlefields.com) and the site of the Gallipoli Association at www.gallipoli-association.org. Other major areas of conflict on land and sea, e.g. the Salonika, East Africa and Mesopotamian fronts, also have dedicated sites and some have their own study societies (such as the Salonika Society at www.salonika.freeserve.co.uk.).

The campaigns and armed forces (Army, Navy, aerial and others) of the Second World War are well covered, most easily via general search engines, though they have not yet attracted as much dedicated interest on the

Internet as the First World War – for the moment. 'Battlefields of World War 2' (battlefieldsww2.50megs.com) has useful information on a range of campaigns and issues and 'D-Day Ancestors' (www.ddayancestors.com) has information on D-Day casualties, war cemeteries and grave locations.

Post-war campaigns are perhaps too recent to have produced such detailed sites or family history interest, though there are old comrades and reunion sites for all sorts of formations – ships, squadrons and regiments – available via search engines. One useful exception is www.britains-smallwars.com which offers information on Britain's post-Second World War operations from Palestine, Malaya, the Korean War, the Falklands and others through to recent operations such as those in the Balkans, Northern Ireland and Sierra Leone. Information on many will also be found via the general search engines.

Sites covering orders, decorations and medals are plentiful and some are excellent. The main collectors' and study group for these items is the Orders and Medals Research Society (www.omrs.org.uk), which produces regular journals. Its American equivalent, the Orders and Medals Society of America (OMSA at www.omsa.org), is also very good. General sites worth considering for information on the basic types of decorations, medals, ribbons etc. are www.medal.net, a very useful site that serves as a portal or link to many other informative locations, and 'Medals of the World' (www.medals.org.uk), which does as its name implies – identifies and details medals and ribbons from all over the world. More detailed specialist sites are available for some of the higher ranking gallantry awards, such as the excellent Victoria Cross websites www.victoriacross.org.uk and www.victoriacross.net. Other award-specific sites (e.g. on the George Cross) can be located simply by using search engines. Life-saving awards are the special subject of the Life Saving Awards Research Society (www.lsars.pwp.blueyonder.co.uk).

For some citations (especially 1914–18), dates of award and other military matters like appointments and promotions within all the services, the *London Gazette* website (www.gazettes-online.co.uk, which can be searched for individuals, campaign dispatches, award citations, promotions etc.) is essential.

It is perhaps unnecessary to state that the Internet is even now only at the beginning of its development as a potential research tool; it can only grow in scope as time passes. For a comprehensive guide to what is currently available to military historians (though largely on Army matters) and family researchers in this field, readers should consult *Researching British Military*

History on the Internet, Dr S C Blank (Paignton, Alwyn Enterprises Ltd, 2007). Apart from this, there is no substitute for actually trawling the net using as many search terms or descriptors as possible; what can be found on even the most obscure military topics is often quite remarkable and is a great testimony to the expertise of institutions and societies and the dedication of countless individuals.

GENERAL BIBLIOGRAPHY

Books on medals have been published since the earliest days of the hobby and some of the nineteenth-century studies are still useful (e.g. J H Mayo, *Medals and Decorations of the British Army and Navy*, Westminster, Archibald Constable & Co., 1897). Although the originals are now collectors' items, many have been reprinted, one good example being Thomas Carter and W H Long, *War Medals of the British Army*, originally printed 1893, reprinted London, Arms & Armour Press, 1972. For a detailed bibliography of orders, decorations and medals, see C P Mulder and A A Purves, *Bibliography of Orders and Decorations*, Copenhagen, Ordenshistorisk Selskab, 1999. The following are more recent general works on medals and research, in addition to those listed within the sections above.

Alexander, E G M, G K B Barron and A J Bateman. *South African Orders, Decorations & Medals*, Cape Town, Human & Rousseau, 1986

Birch, D, J Hayward and R Bishop. *British Battles and Medals*, London, Spink, 2006: this is the essential reference work on British campaign medals

Blatherwick, Surgn Cdr F J. *Canadian Orders, Decorations and Medals*, Toronto, Unitrade Press, 1994

Bowyer, C. *The Air VCs*, London, Kimber, 1978

Campion, R. *Police Medals of the World*, n.p., 2002

Clarke, J D. *Gallantry Medals and Awards of the World*, Sparkford, Patrick Stephens, 1993

Douglas-Morris, Capt. J K. *Naval Medals 1793–1856*, privately published, 1987

Douglas-Morris, Capt. J K. *Naval Medals 1857–1880*, privately published, 1994

Dymond, S. *Researching British Military Medals: A Practical Guide*, Marlborough, Crowood Press, 1999

Farrington, A. *Guide to the Records of the India Office Military Department*, London, India Office Library and Records, 1982

Gordon, Maj. L L. *British Battles and Medals*, 5th edn, London, Spink, 1979

Honours and Awards of the Army, Navy and Air Force, 1914–20, reprint, London, Hayward, 1979

Honours and Awards of the Indian Army, 1914–21, reprint, London, Hayward, 1979

Irwin, R W. *War Medals and Decorations of Canada*, 1969

James, E A. *British Regiments 1914–18*, London, Naval & Military Press, 1993

Kempton, Valour and Gallantry: HEIC and Indian Army VCs and GCs, 1856–1946, Milton Keynes, Military Press, 2001

Laffin, John. *British VCs of World War Two: A Study in Heroism*, Stroud, Budding Books, 2000

Medal Rolls of the Royal Engineers, RE Institute, Chatham: ongoing, several volumes published

Medal Yearbook, Honiton, Token, 2009: published annually

Norman, C B. *Battle Honours of the British Army*, London, John Murray, 1911, reprinted

Oldham, G P and B Delahunt. *Decorations and Medals Awarded to New Zealanders*, Auckland, NZ, G P Oldham, 1991

Poulsom, Maj. N W. *A Catalogue of Campaign and Independence Medals issued during the 20th Century to the British Army*, Minerva, 1969

Prisoners of War: British Army 1939–45, London, HMSO, 1945, reprinted Polstead, Hayward, 1990

Purves, A A. *The Medals, Decorations and Orders of the Great War, 1914–18*, London, Hayward, 1975

Purves, A A. *Collecting Medals and Decorations*, London, Seaby, 1978: useful on many general levels

Purves, A A. *The Medals, Decorations and Orders of World War Two, 1939–45*, Polstead, Hayward, 1986

Rodger, N A M. *Naval Records for Genealogists*, London, HMSO, 1988

Smith, M C. *Awarded for Valour: the History of the Victoria Cross and the Evolution of British Heroism*, Basingstoke, Palgrave Macmillan, 2008

Smyth, Sir J. *The Story of the VC 1856–1963*, London, Muller, 1963

Spencer, W. *Records of the Militia and Volunteer Forces, 1757–1945*, London, PRO, 1998

Spencer, W. *Air Force Records for Family Historians*, London, PRO, 2000

Spencer, William. *Army Service Records of the First World War*, London, PRO, 2001

Spencer, W. *Medals: The Researchers' Guide*, London, TNA, 2007: an essential guide to TNA records

Taprell-Dorling, Capt. H. *Ribbons and Medals*, London, George Philip, 1963, reprinted 1983

Tucker, S and N L G. *In Adversity: Exploits of Gallantry and Awards to the RAF Regiment and its Associated Forces, 1921–95*, n.p., 1997

Williamson, H. *The Collector and Researchers' Guide to the Great War*, Vol. I, privately published, 2003

INDEX